WALKS OF DISCOVERY
IN
SLIEVE BLOOM

by

Thomas P. Joyce

i

I.S.B.N. 0-86335-019-4

Maps reproduced with the permission of
Laois and Offaly County Councils

Published by Thomas P. Joyce
in association with
The Leinster Express

Ye who love the haunts of nature,
Love the sunshine of the meadow,
Love the shadow of the forest,
Love the wind among the branches,
And the rain shower and the snow storm,
And the rushing of great rivers
Through their palisades of pine-trees,
And the thunder in the mountains,
Whose innumerable echoes
Flap like eagles in their eyries ; —
Listen to these wild traditions ....

Henry Wadsworth Longfellow.
'The Song of Hiawatha'

CONTENTS

INTRODUCTION

There is an ever growing interest in walking, and an increasing desire among people to feel close to nature and to know more about the natural order of things and so the aim of this book is to share the pleasures of Slieve Bloom with those who share my interest in the natural world.

How these mountains got their name is not known. Slieve Bloom is the English translation of Sliabh Bladhma and we know that 'sliabh' means 'mountain'. However the meaning of 'Bladhma' is lost, and has been lost for many hundreds of years. In the Book of Leinster, in a poem, an attempt is made to tease out a meaning from the old celtic mythology, but it is inconclusive. We must resign ourselves to the fact that Bladhma is the name, but the meaning, lost in the mists of time, will remain a mystery.

In choosing these walks I wanted the walker to experience what Slieve Bloom has to offer, the sheltered valleys, the rivers, the exposed high moorland, the forestry plantations. Underfoot, to feel the deep heather, the yielding gravel track, the soft bog, the hard tarred road, to cross streams, with bridges, and without bridges. I wanted the walker, at times, to feel far from civilization, alone, in touch, then feel too close to that same civilization, to see how people in the past used the land and how they lived, and how they live and use it now.

Each of these walks is like a string of pearls; some of the pearls are obvious, some not so obvious, all are beautiful, and worth the effort to seek them out.

I have been exploring Slieve Bloom since 1978, and living here since 1981, and the more I discover, the more I realise that I will never discover it all; its beauty is amazing, its story endless.

If you, like most users of Slieve Bloom, walk short distances, preferring circular walks that can be covered in an afternoon, then this book is for you. Many of these short walks can be extended to twice their length, and extended more, and more, to suit yourself.

Remember that on any walk, the pace, distance and difficulty must be suited to the slowest member of the party, so if you are walking with an eight year old (or an eighty year old !) you can only cover a distance suitable for an eight year old, at an eight year old's pace.

With this in mind, I have avoided giving any times for the walks. However, I have given distance, and over the years I have found that an allowance of one hour per mile will prove a good standard.

Some of the walks involve crossing rough terrain, at a height over one thousand feet. For these walks you are advised to wear stout footwear, which gives support to the ankles, bring waterproofs (for protection from the wind as much as the rain) and avoid wearing denims, which have no insulating properties when wet. Always bring a compass and a 'lunch'. Bear in mind that there will be a drop of 2-3 degrees Celcius, for each 300m (1000 feet) of ascent; wind speed (and consequent wind chill) will also increase by 2-3 times; there is 3 times more rain in the mountains, and that on 3 out of 5 days there will be mist on the hills. As a general rule, be comfortable, warm and waterproof.

In preparing the text for each walk I have endeavoured to avoid the complexities of navigation, and to make the 'directions' as simple as possible. I have used just 8 points of the compass, (north, south, east and west, and northeast, northwest, southeast and southwest) and while these are general directions, they will prove adequate when used in conjunction with a good compass and the maps that accompany each walk.

With regard to maps and compass, I recommend you use the Slieve Bloom Environment Park Map (available from Laois and Offaly County Councils, and all local tourist offices) and a 'Silva' compass (available from all good 'outdoor' shops). The compass **(which I regard as essential equipment)** may seem expensive, but it is a precision instrument, and with care, will last a lifetime.

Despite the inconvenience, I would recommend that you bring an illustrated book on flowers, mosses, lichens, birds, or whatever. Whichever you choose you will be well rewarded for the effort of carrying it.

Finally, remember we only have this landscape on loan, it must be handed back as good as, or better than, we found it - take nothing but photographs, and leave nothing but footprints.

Tom Joyce

Glenbarrow, 1995.

FOREWORD

In the 18th. century, the English poet Thomas Hood explored the nature of wild places in a wonderful sonnet called 'Silence'. He distinguished the silence of wilderness, land which has never been shaped by the hand of man, *'where hath been no sound'* or *'where no sound may be'* :

> *In the cold grave - under the deep sea,*
> *Or in wide desert where no life is found*

- from those places which were moulded by the toil and aesthetic instincts of human generations before ours, but from which the tide of human effort has now withdrawn. For Hood, this is the deeper silence, a silence with layers of meaning that our restless spirit may search out and get in touch with

> *...in green ruins, in the desolate walls*
> *Of antique places, where Man hath been,*
> *Though the dun fox, or wild hyena, calls,*
> *And owls, that flit continually between,*
> *Shreik to the echo, and the low winds moan,*
> *There the true Silence is, self - consious and alone.*

For all that, it has become so noisy in our time, this is the silence of Ireland's lonely places. We are an island; people have been living here for over 9,000 years, and there are few places on the island where the human shadow has not fallen.

The first people of the Midlands, gathered around their hunter-fisherfolk campfires on the margins of the lakes which dominated their landscape before the bogs began to grow in their place knew Slieve Bloom, for it was the southern boundary of their world. But we do not know by what name they called it; nor do we know what meaning its surviving name carried for those who first called it so. The earliest human thoughts and memories of these mountains are lost beyond recall.

In the years before the Famines of the 1840's the cultural imprint on the landscape of Slieve Bloom reached its spring tide. The century and a half since then have seen that tide recede. Most of the land reclaimed from the bog and heath, not just over centuries but over millennia, has been given over to evergreen monoculture forest, or has reverted to rushland and scrub. The farmsteads, which carried the human touch to the tops of the valleys and into the mountain's heart, have crumbled to ruin or been swallowed by the advancing forest. The echoes of vanished laughter and conversation are now the merest whisper in the atoms of the rocks at the core of the hills. Tracks and pathways shaped over centuries and kept open by farm traffic and the constant movement of a community which did its keeping-in-touch on foot rather than wheels, are known only to badger, fox and deer. Much of the land has been reclaimed by nature, which has sometimes found new places for itself in that process of recovery; for all that, so much has been lost of the natural inheritance and cultural fabric of the mountains.

But change has always been the way of the landscape: it is like a *palimpsest*. In the early days of writing, a palimpsest was a piece of vellum on which a message would be engraved. But in the days before cheap paper, the expensive vellum would be recycled; the old message rubbed out and a new one engraved, which in turn would also be erased: and so it went on, over and over. But although the obvious message on the vellum would always be the most recent, if you held it to the light in a certain way, you could decipher sentences from earlier messages, and even the odd word or letter of the ones which were written first. So it is for those who learn to decipher and read the landscape in which we live. Underneath the colours, shapes and forms of today, which will in turn be gone tomorrow, are corners and features from every age of the human past, side by side with small and often hidden corners where something of the ancient natural inheritance still finds a place. Every detail of the ground is a relic of human endeavour; things we meet on each walk reflect the human influence at every level, extending in time from the present back to the human beginning: the pine stumps on Knockanastsumba are all that remain of woods in which the first farmers hunted; the tiny willowherb *Epillobium brunnescens*, which is now to be found everywhere at the side of wet tracks and rocky streams in Slieve Bloom, has made its way to us with human help all the way from New Zealand within the last fifty years or so.

In 1854 the great Duwamish Chief Seattle, wrote a wonderful letter to the American President which is often quoted nowadays as an example of how we should relate to the natural world. In it he said that the spirits of his people would always haunt the land which was once their home, and whose air they breathed. It is no different with this land.

What this wonderful book seeks to achieve is to lead the unsuspecting explorer into this land where the modern fabric that hides the wonder of the human past and the more remote past of the natural world is more frayed and rent than most. It is a key that teaches us how to read the palimsest which is the land of Slieve Bloom; showing the way to find our own link with all the wonders of human time and natural diversity. So you must not get the impression that when you have read through these pages and 'done' the walks you are finished with this book. It is hard-covered and pocket-sized for a reason. Every detail along the Way: every flower, each stone and wayside bank has its story; as time goes by other books will weigh down other pockets as your experience of these Ways matures and the colour deepens - books on fungi, flowers, cultural details, and a notebook for your own reflections and observations.

Tom Joyce has chosen the Ways to the heart of Slieve Bloom that will best enable the explorer to find the mountain and to hear its song. It is not a random selection. These are routes planned with much thought and care, the routes that will bring the visitor closest to where the arteries of the mountain can be heard to murmur. There is a wily magic in the innocence of this selection. I don't know whether Tom is secretly a disciple of the Chinese painter Chiang Yee, who wrote a series of short travel books whose innocent everyday prose conceals a mystic response to landscape. There is something of that between these pages, because it is not simply another visitor's guide. It is not incidental that Tom Joyce is a painter and teacher, whose home and spiritual roots extend deep into Slieve Bloom. The book offers you more than clear and accurate information on the Way to walk, and concise and simple explanations of what there is to find; it is as if the text corresponds to the hexagrams of the ancient Chinese diviners; condensed bundles of meanings which unfold as understanding and experience grow, and which become deeper in colour and scent as time goes by.

John Feehan,
Syngefield,
May 1995.

ACKNOWLEDGEMENTS

Over the many years that this book has been germinating, countless people have assisted in one way or another (many unaware of how important that assistance was) some have given time, advice and information, some have uttered encouraging words at critical times, others have listened; all have helped the seed to sprout and flower. My most sincere thanks to ....

my wife Anne; my patient children; even more patient Helena; John Feehan; James Scully; Michael Byrne; Richard, Betty and Andrew Gray. My friends in Coillte: Richard Jack, Joe Clancy, Pat O'Brien, John Snell and Dermot O'Brien; Cait Kavanagh and the staff in Laois County Library. Jerry Lodge, Niall Bradley and Louis Brennan in Laois County Council; Sean McCarthy in Offaly County Council; Eddie and Nan Troy, Clonaslee; Frank and Angela Thomas, Tullamore, and Martin Connolly of Imperial Print & Design, who took such a personal and professional interest in the book.

For essential help, my thanks to
Laois County Council
Offaly Enterprise Board
National Heritage Council
Powers Gold Label Irish Whiskey
Lowe Alpine Systems, Tullamore
Tullamore Nature Rambling Society
Gray Insurances Ltd., Tullamore.

Patrons of the Book

Josephine Elliffe, Arden View, Tullamore,
Michael McGrath, Pearse Park, Tullamore,
Sherwood Medical Industries, Sragh, Tullamore
Telford Ltd., Mountrath & Portlaoise
'Dan & Molly's', Ballyboy, Kilcormac
Edmund Dunne, The Lodge, Clonaslee
Derry Kilroy, Paddy Dolan, Conor Donnelly, Mike Flynn,
Dick Whelehan High St., Tullamore
Sweeneys Mace Supermarket, Clonaslee
Richard & Betty Gray, Sragh, Tullamore
Noel Foynes, Clonaslee
Tullamore Credit Union, Patrick St., Tullamore
Fergal McCourt, Coneyboro, Celbridge
Dympna & Michael Thunder, Flower Grove, Dunlaoire
Tom & Renee Harney, Charleville View, Tullamore
Mai Choiseul, Spollenstown, Tullamore
Dr. Morgan Flynn, Tyrrellspass
Maree Kelly, Tyrrellspass
W. J. Keegan Ltd., Auctioneers, Church St., Tullamore
Bank of Ireland, Tullamore
Paddy Cunniffe, Arbutus Court, Tullamore
Maeve & Malachy Mangan, Castlebarnagh, Daingean
Pat Bolger, Bank of Ireland, Mountrath
John Lee, Stragelliffe, Cavan
Sheila Igoe, Charleville Ave., Tullamore
Tom Farrell & Partners, Solicitors, O'Connor Sq., Tullamore
Dr. Aidan Hanson, Mountmellick
Marius & Sylvia Aregger, Zurich
Donal & Evelyn Hogan, Banagher
George Campion, Clara Rd., Tullamore
Canice & Maura Sheeran, The Village Inn, Coolrain
Charles Flannagan T.D., Stradbally Rd., Portlaoise
Martin Connolly, Derryguile, Portlaoise
Particia Quinn, Clara House, Clara

Kirwan's Camping & Caravan Park, Portlaoise
Peter Quinn, Crowley Millar Solicitors, Dublin
Margaret Daly, Unisex Hair Salon, Portlaoise
Seamus Sexton, Mountmellick
Marie & Tom Tracey, The Heath, Portlaoise
Paul Daly, Shane, Portlaoise
Malachy Scally, Monkstown Group, Foxrock, Dublin
Arnold Fanning, Midland Tribune, Birr
Declan & Clare Kirrane, Killenard, Portarlington
Kevin O'Hora, Lea Rd., Portarlington
Olive Slevin, Killenard, Portarlington
Noel Maher, St.Paul's Secondary School, Monasterevin
Brid Broderick, Arden Rd., Tullamore
Linda Dowling & Aidan Barry, Clara Rd., Tullamore
Christina Collier, Station Rd., Portarlington
Val & Mary Hughes, Arden Vale, Tullamore
Angela & Frank Thomas, Arden Rd., Tullamore
Sean Wrafter, Harbour St., Tullamore
Noel & Teresa Lally, Church St., Tullamore
Tommy Moore, Convent Rd., Tullamore
Maura Behan, Kilmullen House, Portarlington
Anne Kingston, Rushin Rd., Mountrath
Marcus & Jane Farrell, Sragh, Tullamore
Brendan Morgan, Spollenstown, Tullamore
Dominic & Marguerite Madden, New Rd., Tullamore
Offaly Historical & Archaeological Society, Tullamore
Vanessa & Will Fennelly, Clonminch, Tullamore
Tony & Liz Holleran, Whitehall Est., Ttullamore
Paddy & Anne Egan, Ballyvora, Ferbane
Nancy & Gabriel Harrison, Clara Rd., Tullamore
Jimmy Hughes, Main St., Clara
Patsy & Nancy Thomas, Pearse Park, Tullamore
William Telford, Mountrath
Thomas J. Wrafter, Church St., Tullamore
John & Margaret Brady, Main St., Daingean
Mairead Wrenn, Rahan Rd., Tullamore

Gary & Kay Kilroy, Middleton Park, Castletowngeoghan
John Dollard, Monacurragh, Carlow
Milne O'Dwyer & Co., Kilbride St., Tullamore
Maree McElduff, Hophill Grove, Tullamore
Margaret Dollard, Circular Rd., Kilkenny
Liam & Sara Stapleton, Cloonagh, Mountmellick
Pat Donnelly, Arden Vale, Tullamore
Liam & Dolores Hoctor, Arden Heights, Tullamore
Michael & Geraldine Byrne, Convent View, Tullamore
Tom & Mary Roche, Arden Vale, Tullamore
Matt Dunne & Associates Auctioneers, Portarlington
Percy & Phil Clendennan, 'Giltraps', Kinnitty
Olive Milne, Crinkle, Birr
Marie Collins, Monasterevin
Mary Byrne, Dove Grove, Birr
Christina Byrne, Ardmore House, Kinnitty
Pat & Mary Finn, Carrowmanagh, Lusmagh, Banagher
Eileen Mooney, Clontarf Rd., Tullamore
James Scully, Meelick, Eyrecourt
Gerard Moriarty, Irish Times, Belfast
Michael Parsons, Collier's Lane, Portlaoise
Eddie & Eileen Hill, Langton Rd., Newbridge
Frank & Marita Nicholson, Charleville Rd., Tullamore
Williams Waller Ltd., Patrick St., Tullamore
Celene & Fran Simpson, Ballycarroll, Portarlington
Catherine Longworth, New Rd., Tullamore
Kevin McMahon, Whitehall Est., Tullamore
Lucy, Louis, Brad, Conor & Emily
Tom McGee, Attinkee, Banagher
John & Dolores Scully, Elmfield, Spollenstown, Tullamore
Offaly County Council Social Club, Courthouse, Tullamore
Frank & Rosemarie Kennan, Roundwood House, Mountrath
Pauline Buggy, The Village, Portlaoise
John P. Buggy, Portlaoise
Laurie & Deborah Grey, Ross, Screggan, Tullamore
The Joyce Family, High Street, Tullamore

ILLUSTRATIONS

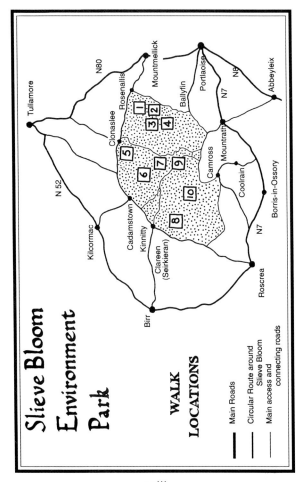

Slieve Bloom Environment Park

WALK LOCATIONS

Main Roads

Circular Route around Slieve Bloom

Main access and connecting roads

LEGEND FOR SKETCH MAPS OF
WALKS 1-10

COUNTY ROAD

FOREST TRACK

WALK ROUTE

FOREST BOUNDARY
(Often with fence)

TURF BANKS

START OF WALK

CONIFEROUS TREES

DECIDUOUS TREES

WATERFALL

BRIDGE

RIVER
(and direction of flow)

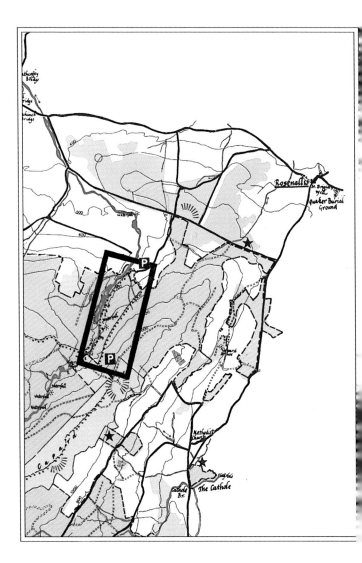

<u>Walk 1</u>
<u>Glenbarrow River Valley - 3km</u>
<u>(2miles)</u>

     This circular walk will take you along the eastern bank of the river Barrow on a very obvious track through a most interesting riverside landscape, returning to the start along gravel forest roads through a plantation of varying age.

     To get to Glenbarrow from Rosenallis, take the road for Clonaslee, or Mountrath, and follow signposts for Glenbarrow.

     From Clonaslee take the road to Rosenallis and after 3km (2 miles) turn off to the right following signposts for Glenbarrow.

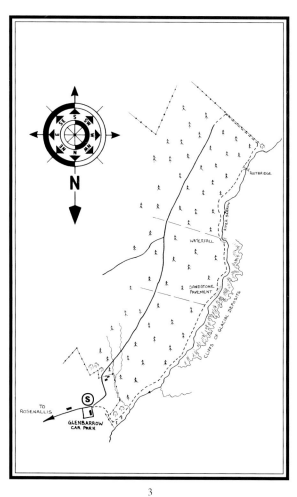

N

FOOTBRIDGE

RIVER BARROW

WATERFALL

SANDSTONE
PAVEMENT

CLIFFS OF GLACIAL DEPOSITS

TO
ROSENALLIS

(S)

GLENBARROW
CAR PARK

__Starting at the car park in Glenbarrow, descend by the path on the right, signposted Tinnahinch 3km. At the bottom of the path pass through the timber gate on the left leading into the forest plantation.__

Here the beech trees help to soften the hard edge of the plantation. The contrast between the bare forest floor on the right and the abundance of plant life on the left, illustrates how ecologically rich a deciduous woodland is in comparison to a coniferous one.

Because sunlight is essential for the growth of all green plants, the close planting of the coniferous trees ensures that as they grow, their lower branches die in the shade; this helps to reduce the knots in the harvested timber and forces the tree to reach higher for the light, helping to keep its trunk straight. The absence of light at the forest floor eliminates all other green plants which would compete for the nutrients in the soil.

As you continue along the path, you will notice places where light does reach the forest floor, and here there will be some grasses, ferns, and brambles.

However don't think that this forest floor is dead - in autumn it is a mass of all sorts of fungi that grow on decaying timber and among the carpet of pine needles.

Where the forest has been harvested, all the plants and seeds that had been dormant, reawaken and compete with each other to cover the ground as quickly as possible.

As you walk along the path, occasionally you will find spruce and pine cones which have been stripped by the red squirrels that inhabit this woodland. Their sharp teeth easily chop through the tough scales to get to the seeds behind.

In all my rambles through Slieve Bloom, I have never seen the Grey Squirrel, though I believe they have been seen in the Kinnitty area. The Grey Squirrel is larger than the Red and has a more diverse diet, so when in competition for food and territory, the Grey can easily displace the native Red.

After approx. 800m (0.5 miles) you will come to the large open area by the river where the stone floor of the valley is exposed. This rock is sandstone and it started as grains of sand in the bed of a huge river, which

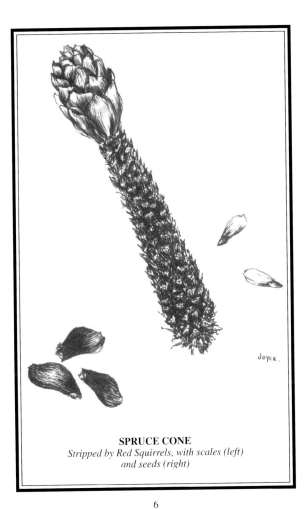

SPRUCE CONE
*Stripped by Red Squirrels, with scales (left)
and seeds (right)*

flowed through this part of the world some 380 million years ago !

Eventually these grains of sand were compacted and compressed into stone. Because sandstone forms in layers, it splits easily into regular flags, and this place, though now looking as though untouched through time, was in fact a quarry in the last century. It is said that the quarry was abandoned after a local man was killed in a blasting accident.

If you go down onto the sandstone pavement and examine the small cliff, you will clearly see the layering of the sandstone, and an examination of the cliff base will reveal the bore holes for the explosive used to blast the rock, and high up to the left, the initials of those men who worked here.

The bottoms of other boreholes can be seen in the pavement nearby.

On the opposite side of the river the impressive cliffs are the legacy of the last Ice Age. Over 10,000 years ago, as the huge ice sheet, which had crept into the valleys and over the northern slopes of Slieve Bloom, began to melt, the debris it had picked up (from as far away as Galway) covered the

PAVEMENT QUARRY IN GLENBARROW

slopes and choked the valleys. Nowhere in Slieve Bloom is this glacial till so well displayed as here in Glenbarrow.

Following the path upriver, you come to the Clamphole Falls. Here, beneath the sandstone, is a layer of softer reddish rock called mudrock. As the soft mudrock was steadily eroded away, the overlying sandstone could not support its own weight and collapsed into the river, creating a waterfall. The large boulders in the river below the waterfall were once this overhanging sandstone.

Follow the path past the waterfall, and after approx. 400m you will come to the timber footbridge over the river. Do not cross the bridge, but continue on the track to the end of the forest plantation, where you turn left and begin to ascend along the edge of the forest .

As you get higher up the slope you will have a fine view of upper Glenbarrow and the townland of Cones, at the head of the valley.

After ascending for approx. 300m, watch for the Slieve Bloom Way turning marker in the middle of the track and at the

marker, turn left along a short, rough track through the trees. At the end of this track you meet the forest road which will lead you back to Glenbarrow car park.

When walking along the road, watch for the footprints of the fallow deer that inhabit this area. As they walk, or casually trot along, fallow deer place the hind hoofs (called cleaves) in, or almost in, the place of the fore cleaves, giving rise to double footprints. Very occasionally you will find fine clear prints and it is worth considering making plaster casts of these. This can be a fascinating (and educational) pastime, which adds a whole new dimension to your walks. The casts can become an interesting collection, and with a bit of imagination, make most unusual wall mountings.

Less than 800m (0.5 miles) farther on, another forest road leads off to the right, ignore this road and continue downhill.

This area was clearfelled between 1990 and 1993 and well illustrates how quickly the bare forest floor is reclaimed by the plants, once the trees are removed.

FOOTPRINTS OF FALLOW DEER

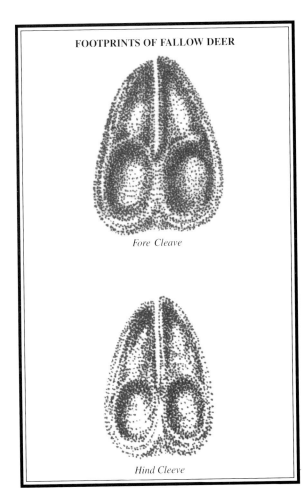

Fore Cleave

Hind Cleave

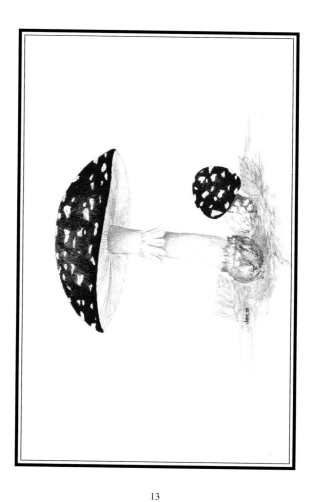

As you descend along the road there is a fine panoramic view of the flat land to the north, with the bogs of Annaghmore and Monettia, and the stump of the long extinct volcano that is now Croghan Hill. Binoculars will reveal the tower of Charleville Castle and the spire of the Roman Catholic church in Tullamore, under which I once lived.

Soon you reach the gate at the end of the forest plantation and if it is late summer or autumn, then under the birch trees on the right, you will find splendid examples of the 'Fly Agaric' fungus *Amanita muscaria* (the toadstool most often favoured by illustrators of children's fairy stories) but be careful it is very poisonous, though unlikely to be fatal. In the 13th. century Albertus Magnus, the outstanding German philosopher and natural scientist, recommended it broken up in milk, as a fly killer, hence the name.

Another 150m along the lane and you will be back in the car park.

Walk 2
Ridge of Capard - 5.5km
(3.5 miles)

Without doubt this is the finest ridge walk in Slieve Bloom, providing a variety of underfoot conditions, wonderful views to the east and south and the opportunity to come really close to the plant life of the blanket bog.

Starting at the car park on the Ridge of Capard, the walk follows the route of the Slieve Bloom Way over the blanket bog as far as the cairn on the ridge, known locally as The Stoney Man. From the cairn you will descend into Glenbarrow valley, to meet a forest road which leads back to the car park.

This is one of the walks which involves crossing very rough and rugged terrain at a height <u>over</u> 300m (1000 feet) and you would be well advised to wear stout footwear and to bring waterproofs.

To get to the start from Rosenallis take the road for Mountrath and follow signposts for the Ridge of Capard.

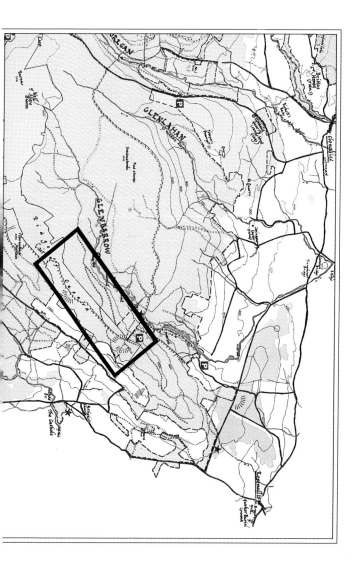

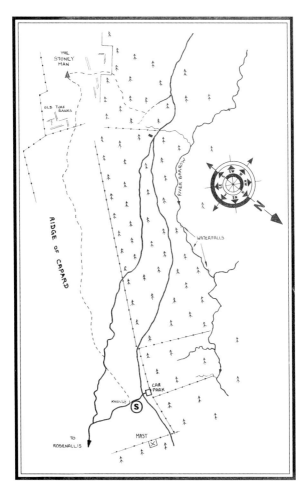

Park beyond the picnic table and seats at the top of the ridge.

Begin your walk at the picnic table ascending through the heather, past the marker for the Slieve Bloom Way.

After 100m stop and get your bearings.

Ahead of you, to the southwest, stretches the ridge, and if visibility is good you will see the cairn in the distance. From here it looks small, but it is over 2.5m high !

To the right is the forest plantation through which you will return, and behind you is the communications mast (known locally as The Metal Man).

Continue on a track through the heather for approx. 400m to meet a forest road. Already you will appreciate the hard surface underfoot, enjoy it while you can, soon you will be back in the heather !

Continue along the road for about 70m, keeping a watch for the Slieve Bloom Way marker on the left hand side. At this marker leave the track and start out for one in the series of poles, which are positioned at intervals along the ridge to aid walkers when visibility is bad (usually about 200 days

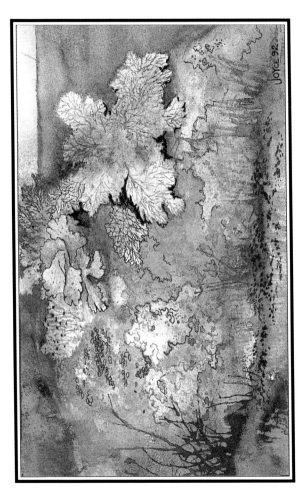

19

in the year).

There is no clearly defined route between one pole and the next so wander and ramble as you wish, to choose the most interesting, or easiest way.

Some people might regard this landscape as barren and bleak, but while trees and shrubs would have a hard time surviving here, this is a most fascinating place, producing thousands of small plants, each beautiful in its own right.

Explore this wonderland at your feet and you will discover that amazing family of lichens, Cladonia. If you have brought a book on lichens you will have no difficulty identifying *Cladonia portentosa*, growing in clumps amongst the heather. Its multi branched stems have a delicate pale green colour. It contains the antibiotic, usnic acid, and was once used to dye woolens yellow. *Cladonia floerkeana*, often called matchstick lichen, because of the conspicuous red tips on its stalks. These lichens bear witness to the purity of the air.

Another family that you should become acquainted with, are the mosses Sphagnum.

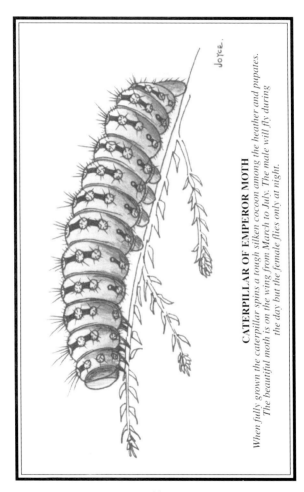

CATERPILLAR OF EMPEROR MOTH

When fully grown the caterpillar spins a tough silken cocoon among the heather and pupates. The beautiful moth is on the wing from March to July. The male will fly during the day but the female flies only at night.

These mosses are all important to this landscape : without them there would be no blanket bog. Sphagnum has had a variety of uses over the years. Because of its capacity to absorb and store water, (90% of its bulk is water) it was used in the past for 'nappies' and sanitary towels, and in the First World War, for field dressings. Today, Bord na Mona is investigating the use of sphagnum peat fibre for these same sanitary purposes, and has already developed sphagnum fibre to replace existing, expensive charcoal filters, and for the treatment of sewage effluent.

With a book, you should easily identify *Sphagnum capillifolium*, growing in compact crimson red clumps, and *Sphagnum papillosum*, usually a yellowish green, and found in the wetter places.

These are only a few of the many, many plants and no matter how often I walk on this mountain, I am fascinated by their diversity and variety.

As you near the Stoney Man, you will have the comfort of walking on a track, which leads through a gate, and almost right up to the cairn. This was the track to the

mountain bog, where many of the families who lived in Glenbarrow, and on the eastern side of the ridge, harvested their fuel from turf banks which, though now cloaked in heather, are still discernible in the landscape.

At the cairn you will find shelter from the wind in the hollow behind. This place was once a quarry, and if you have time to kill, or a lunch to eat, there is no nicer place to stop on this walk, than here. Sit down, relax, enjoy the panorama, and try to remember the names and faces of your new acquaintances, be they Cladonias or Sphagnums ! If visibility is good you will see the Wicklow mountains to the east, the Blackstairs to the southeast, and north, as far as the eye can see.

The cairn, which is the finest and best maintained I have seen in any mountain range, is built from the discarded stone of this long abandoned quarry and its maintenance is the responsibility of all who pass here.

When leaving the cairn head northwest over the heather, which as you descend into the Barrow valley can be knee deep in places.

Refer carefully to the sketch map for the walk, to see the limits of the forest

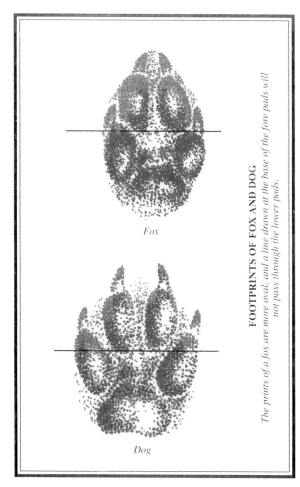

Fox

Dog

FOOTPRINTS OF FOX AND DOG

The prints of a fox are more oval, and a line drawn at the base of the fore pads will not pass through the lower pads.

plantation ahead, and the easiest route to the forest road in the valley. Though not immediately obvious, in places the plantation is sparsely planted, and there is an easy line of descent through open ground to the gravel forest road.

When you reach the road turn right, heading northeast, down the valley towards the more mature forest plantation. Shortly after entering the plantation you come to a forest road junction. Here you will be taking the road to the left. However, just before the junction, on the right, at the edge of the road, surrounded by spruce trees, is the ruin of a cottage (the last house in the valley) once occupied by a family by the name of Clear. In the 'Big Snow' of 1947, the family had to be rescued by their neighbours, who literally had to dig them out of this cottage. It was recorded that the snow was up to the eaves, and only the chimney distinguished the house from its surroundings. The family moved down from the mountains to lower, better ground in the early 1960's and still live in the area.

From the junction, the road winds its way through the plantation, back to the car

DROPPINGS OF FOX AND PINE MARTEN

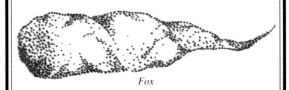

Fox

Fox droppings are generally black in colour, turning grey as they get older and have a long sharp point. Often containing bits of bone, feathers and fur. In the autumn the droppings may appear blue or blackish, indicating that the fox was eating blackberries. The droppings of the Pine Marten have a strong, foul smell and are spirally twisted, ending in a long point. Fresh droppings are shiny and black.

Pine Marten

**park at the top of the ridge.**

As you walk, keep a watch for the prints
and droppings of deer, badger, fox and pine
marten, because while roads through
plantations are primarily for the maintenance
of the forest, and later the extraction of the
timber, they serve as major highways for the
wildlife of the area, by day and by night.

Walk 3
Tinnahinch - 7km (4.4 miles)

This circular walk will take you along forest roads and over the blanket bog of Knocknastumba, and will give you an insight into Slieve Bloom's past character.

The roads are firm and provide easy walking, and in fine weather, a pair of comfortable walking shoes, or good runners, are adequate for these. However, the moorland is rough, and I would recommend strong footwear (walking boots or similar) which gives support to the ankles.

At 400m (1300 feet) the open moorland is exposed and windswept, so bring protection from the wind and rain. As always, bring a book on mosses, lichens, fungi, flowers, grasses, or whatever - when your walk is over, and you are sitting at the fire, be it at home, or in the pub, it will add to your satisfaction to know that you have become familiar with one or two more plants in the area.

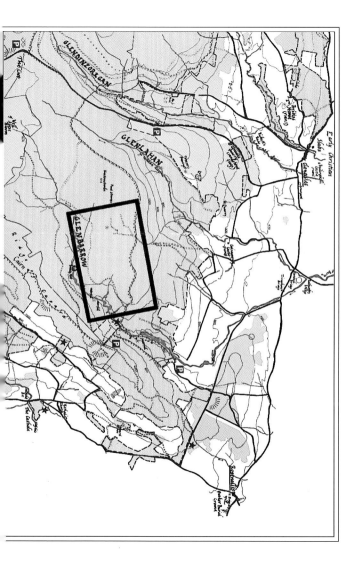

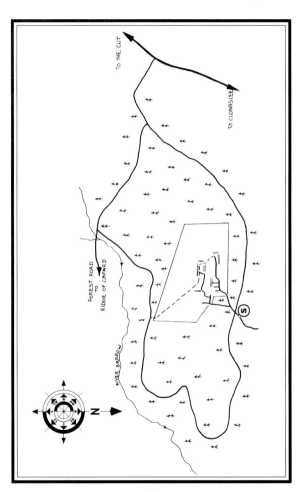

TO THE CUT

TO CLONASLEE

FOREST ROAD
TO
RIDGE OF CAPARD

RIVER BARROW

S

N

To get to the start of the walk, drive for 5.6km (3.5 miles) from Clonaslee up the road to the Cut, until you come to a gravel forest road leading off to the left, signposted 'Slieve Bloom Way'.

Leaving the tarred road, drive along this gravel track (beware of the uneven surface) where after about 1.2km (0.7miles) you come to a junction. Keep left, and continue for another 3km (almost 2 miles). Park here, at a small crossroads, which is little more than where two gravel tracks cross.

Begin your walk by taking the track to the right, uphill, through the larch and lodgepole pine plantation, towards the moorland. This is the route taken by generations of families who cut turf on the mountain bog of Tinnahinch.

After a short distance, the track divides into two. Take the branch to the right and continue on this main track until it ends. Ignore all other minor tracks leading off to the left and right.

I have often encountered ravens in this area. If you call to them, with their characteristic 'prruk', they will often reply,

RAVENS OVER TINNAHINCH
Ravens mate for life, and generally use the same nest for many years. This cautious, vigilant bird, which can have a wing span over 1m, can be taught to mimic human speech.

and even come closer to investigate you in greater detail.

At the end of the track, start out, due southeast, uphill, across the open moorland.

The area of turf banks ahead always reminds me of an archaeological site, and I suppose in many respects it is. The turf bank itself is like the side of an archaeological trench, and provides an insight into the climate as well as a record of all that has grown here since the last Ice Age, 10,000 years ago. The now exposed and leached soil and sand beneath the peat, is the decayed, underlying conglomerate and the glacial deposits of that Ice Age, upon which flourished, in turn, juniper, willow, birch and hazel. These trees in turn were replaced by the pines.

As early man cleared pockets of this woodland, the fragile shallow soils were exposed and eroded until eventually (probably triggered by a deterioration to a wetter climate) the first stage in the development of this blanket bog was initiatcd.

The acidic bog, in turn, killed off the pines, and here, beneath the blanket of peat, now exposed as a result of cutting the turf, are the stumps of those pines that grew here so abundantly 5,000 years ago.

You should examine these stumps more closely. On some, beneath a thin crust of peat, you will find the bark of the tree still intact. I have found that touching the beautifully coloured bark of a 5,000 year old Scots Pine puts my own mortality into a new perspective.

It was these stumps, found by the earliest Irish speaking turf cutters, that gave a name to this area, Cnoc na Stumpa - The Hill of the Stumps.

In the more recent past, these naturally preserved and weathered timbers were used as 'mantletrees', and lintels for doors and windows, in many of the old houses and cottages in these parts.

When leaving the cut away bog, head southeast, across the moorland, gradually descending to Glenbarrow.

If you cross the moorland in May or June, you may see large swathes of Cotton Grass (Bog Cotton or Mare's Tail) a sure sign that the heather was burned in the past. As the seeds of Cotton Grass can survive such fires, they quickly take advantage of the cleared

ground to germinate and reproduce.

The deliberate burning of heather was common on this moorland. Tinnahinch mountain was greatly favoured for grouse shooting by its owners, the Dunnes of Brittas, and the shooting rights for Tinnahinch were much sought after.

Young grouse feed on the tender new shoots of young heather, and it was important as part of the maintenance of the grouse moors, that the older clumps of heather be burned back.

However, the uncontrolled burning of heather, and the danger of accidental fire, were constantly feared by the gamekeeper of this moorland, and his employer. Here is the text of a letter from the leasee of the shooting rights to Richard Egan of Tinnahinch, the gamekeeper, who lived about 2km from here....

W.R.Meredith & Son,   32 Molesworth St.,
Solicitors, Land Agents,   Dublin.
Commissioners for Oaths.

                    16th. June 1930.
Dear Egan,
               Many thanks for yours. I am glad
the fire was no worse.
               We have got off very well so far
and I am hoping for a real good season. I hope
its not too dry with you. We're all crying out for
rain here and the county is parched. A fire in
this season could easily burn the whole
mountain if it wasn't got at once. All you can
do is keep your eyes open and warn the turf
cutters that burning heather is illegal at this time
of year.

                              Yours Truly,
                              R.Meredith.

Before you reach the forest track, which
completely encircles Knocknastumba, it will
be necessary to pass through the forest
plantation, which completely surrounds the
open moorland.

__When you reach the forest plantation continue downhill (along the margin of the plantation) searching for the easiest line of descent through the trees to the forest track just 100m below.__

__When you reach the track turn left.__ The distance back to the start, along this track, is approximately 4km (2.5 miles) and the walking is easy. Even if you have no companion with a good story to shorten the road, there will be plenty to interest you along the way.

If the visibility is good, as you approach the start, you should get a fine view of the cooling towers of the E.S.B. power station at Lumcloon, near Ferbane, 24km (15 miles) away in Co.Offaly.

Walk 4
Cones - The Source of the Barrow
5km (3 miles)

In the past, the source of the Barrow was known as 'The Well of Sliabh Bládhma' and it was believed that any interference with it (even to look upon it !) would result in great downpours of rain, which would cause the river to rise up and flow in great torrents through the valley, until the spirit of the well was appeased.

If the Barrow did originate from a 'well' or spring then (like the origin of the name 'Bládhma') it has been lost to us.

After all my wanderings and rambles in the area, I still have not found a distinct and definite source to the Barrow. However, I believe that there once was a 'well', or some known feature.

The Book of Glendalough makes reference to it and says that the floods caused by interfering with it would only abate when,

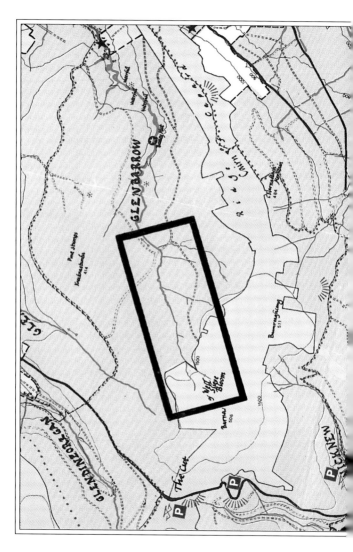

"the offering of the Body of Christ is made at the well". The Norman historian, Giraldus Cambrensis, described how a specially appointed priest *("who from birth has been a virgin in mind and body")* would say this mass of appeasement in a chapel situated nearby. After the mass and *"when he has blessed the waters and sprinkles upon them the milk of a cow of one colour - the well will be appeased".*

It is easy to see the blending of the Pagan and Christian religions in this ceremony, which might perhaps be an indication that the tradition pre-dates Christianity.

We may never know. But if the day is fine, I would suggest that you explore this area known as the "Well of Sliabh Bládhma" and perhaps you will be the one to find the elusive source.

I remember one February morning, after two days and nights of heavy rain, I walked by the riverside path to the Clamphole Falls in Glenbarrow, and believe me, I could appreciate the origins of the myth. It was an unforgettable experience - the river was huge, seething, powerful, angry. Its volume had increased perhaps five fold. It clawed at the banks with a ferocity that was frightening. At the log hut the sandstone pavement was completely covered by many feet of churning water, and I could hear the dull rumble of great rocks being rolled downstream. As I stood there, not logs, but whole trees, washed past me. Just upstream, at the Falls, normally the river flows over three distinct steps, now it cascaded from its upper level, into the plunge pool, in one continuous, roaring mass, its spume filling the air.

It is thought that the Barrow got its name from the Irish word 'beiriú', to boil, and since that February morning I fully subscribe to that theory.

To get to the start of the walk, drive in from the Cut road, along the gravel track, for 1.2 km (0.7 miles) as for Walk 3, but at the junction of the forest roads, turn right, heading southeast into upper Glenbarrow.

After 1.6 km (1 mile) another forest road leads off to the left, park here, at this junction.

You are now in the townland of Cones, a name perhaps derived from the word 'con', meaning wolf or hound, or perhaps from the

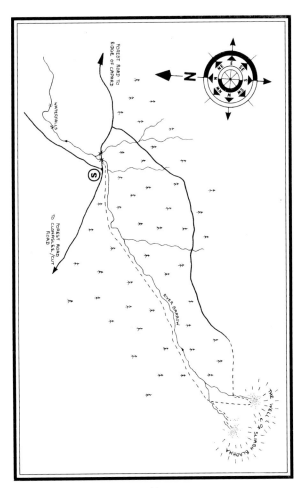

FOREST ROAD TO RIDGE OF CAPPRD

WATERFALLS

N

S

FOREST ROAD TO CLONASLEE/CUT ROAD

RIVER BARROW

THE WELL C. OF SLINGA BLADHMA

appearance of the summits of Clarnahinch, Baunreaghcong, Barna and Wolftrap.

To begin your walk, head southeast along the forest road, descending to the concrete bridge which spans the trickling stream that is the Barrow. It is hard to imagine that this little stream grows into Ireland's second largest river.

Continue on this forest road for another 200m, and take the track to the right, heading south, towards the summit of Baunreaghcong.

This track gradually ascends for 2km (1.25 miles) to the open moorland. As you get higher on the track the whole panorama of Glenbarrow will unfold.

On the track, and at its margins, there is an abundance of plant life, which becomes even more abundant as your height increases and the road deteriorates. It always surprises me that many who enjoy walking in and over landscape such as this, know so few of the plants that are literally under their feet. Quite naturally the colourful flowering plants attract most of our attention, but these moorland plants deserve more recognition than they get.

At the end of the track, head due west (along the edge of the forest plantation) across the blanket bog.

A short distance beyond the end of the plantation, watch carefully for the small stream, almost hidden in the vegetation. Cross the stream and continue uphill, along its western bank, until the stream disappears into the moorland.

If you dare to explore this birthplace of the Barrow then perhaps in a few days you will come back to view the threatened torrent raging through the valley below !

When leaving the depressions at the beginnings of the stream, head due north to meet the other branch of the river. If you wish to explore the source of this branch of the Barrow (which is far more impressive than the other) then continue uphill, along the bank or in the bed of the stream. If you wish to descend, then cross this branch and continue descending, due northeast, between the bank of the river and the forest plantation. As you descend, watch for the paths through the vegetation, made by the deer. These paths meander a bit, but provide

RIVER BARROW GODHEAD
One of the thirteen sculptures representing the principal rivers of Ireland. The work of Edward Smyth, these heads are the keystones on the Custom House in Dublin, designed by James Gandon.

*<u>a sure footed descent through this rough
ground.</u>*

As you descend, you will notice the
extent of sedges and meadow grasses all
around these headwaters. Before this area was
planted with conifers, it had, in the summer
months, a prairie like appearance with its
carpet of grasses. In early Ireland haymaking
was unknown, and this pasture did not go
unnoticed by early Irish farmers, who, with
their herds of cattle, migrated to these upland
pastures for the summer months. This practice
was known as 'booleying', and there is, what
may be, a booley hut, further down the river.

You will also notice the remains of a
stone wall, which in places is on the left bank
of the river and at others, on the right bank.
This wall, built in the last century at a cost of
2d. per man, per day (equal to one penny
today) divided the estates of Capard and
Brittas and it crosses the river to establish the
right of ownership, of each estate, to the water.

**<u>When you reach the concrete bridge at
the forest road, turn left, uphill, to the start
of this Walk.</u>**

Walk 5
Brittas, Clonaslee - 5.6km
(3.5 miles)

This easy, pleasant walk begins in the village of Clonaslee and follows the Clodiagh River upstream through Coill Bhriotais - a mixed open wood; passes Brittas House and continues on forest tracks, past the artificial lake of Brittas Demesne, returning to the village by way of the early 19th. century avenue.

Essential equipment for this walk is a good bird book and binoculars. Apart from its flora, the wood has an amazing variety of birdlife, and if you have a particular interest in ornithology, then you might get no further than the end of the riverside path !

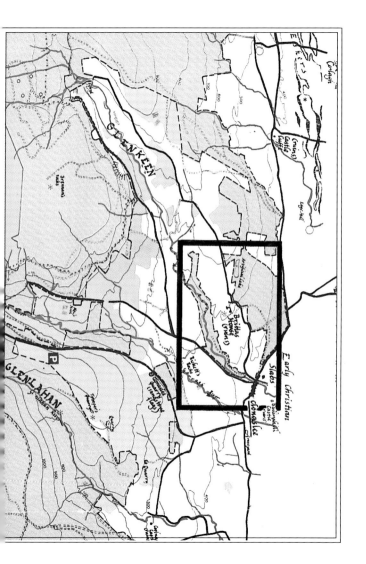

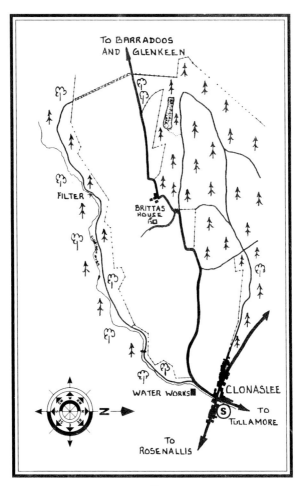

TO BARRADOOS
AND GLENKEEN

FILTER

BRITTAS
HOUSE

WATER WORKS

CLONASLEE

TO
TULLAMORE

TO
ROSENALLIS

S

N

Park in the village, and begin your walk at the bridge over the Clodiagh River. ***At the crossroads take the road due South, between the lodge house and the bridge. A 100 m farther on turn left into Coill an Bhriotais (Brittas Wood).***

As you pass through the forest gate you will notice, on the opposite bank of the river, the reservoir and water works which supplies water to Tullamore.

No matter what the time of year, I think this entrance to the wood, and the approach to the timber footbridge farther on, is a most beautiful place.

Do not cross the footbridge, but continue straight on, past the open field and over the wire fences.

The path winds its way through the trees beside the river for almost a mile and a half, and you will have to cross many of these wire fences on your way. The fences provide access corridors to the river for landowners whose land adjoins the plantation. Some of the fences have steps, while others have the barbs removed from the top strand of wire; but no matter, they are all easy to negotiate.

Immediately after the second set of fences, on the left, is a fine old oak tree upon which grows an abundance of plants : ferns, mosses, lichens, and indeed, high up in a crevice of one of its branches, an ash seedling.

This tree illustrates how the oak, more than any other tree, provides a habitat for other plants and animals, and consequently adds much to the ecological diversity of an area. In the immediate vicinity of this fascinating tree is ash, hazel, beech, holly, birch, willow and sycamore - a place to linger perhaps.

Farther on, at another set of fences, you will notice, on the right of the path, rhododendrons, which 'escaped' from the gardens of Brittas House.

After a time you will come to an intriguing cut-stone structure on the left, at the river. Much overgrown with mosses and small plants, and beech trees growing from its top and side walls, it can be easily missed. On first glance it would appear to be the ruins of a bridge, where the arch has collapsed, but a closer examination will only confuse, rather than confirm this theory.

On the upstream side, in the river, is a

low, beautifully chamfer-cut, sandstone capped wall, in a curving arch that spanned the river.

Some of the dislodged capstones, now in the river, have chiselled sockets, into which lead would have been poured, and metal railings fitted.

This was the filter and grille for a large hydraulic ram used for pumping water, and built by the Dunnes of Brittas. The grille prevented debris washed down in the river from entering the ram, and the wall would have slowed the flow of the river allowing the sediment to settle. The ram itself is farther downstream.

The walls and embankments were in fact part of a bridge for a road that crossed the river and continued on to Brittas House.

__As you approach the end of the plantation, the track curves gently to the right, and rises away from the river to a broad, straight lane. Continue along this lane, which after 400m, meets the tarred road from Clonaslee to the townlands of Glenkeen and Barradoo.__

__At the road, turn downhill towards__

Brittas House. If the day is fine, and visibility is good, the panorama ahead, looking over the northeastern foothills of Slieve Bloom, is a delight. In the distance, you will see the cooling tower of Portarlington power station 26km (16 miles) away, and on the horizon, you might see the mountains of Wicklow. Farther along the road and looking to the northeast, you should see Croghan Hill, near Daingean, the stump of a long extinct volcano.

As you descend along the road you can't but admire the sandstone front walls of the dwellings on the right.

About 60m before the first sharp bend in the road, and about 5m before the first of two sycamore trees, on the right, secured to the wall, and almost hidden by ivy and holly, is a small, rusty, iron cross. During the Civil War in 1922, soldiers of the Irish Republican Army sheltered in the grounds of Brittas House. Their presence was discovered and the castle was attacked be the opposing Free State Army. When darkness came most escaped across the fields to Brittas Wood. However, one of their number, a young man of 22 years, named Seamus Phelan, from Mountrath, tried

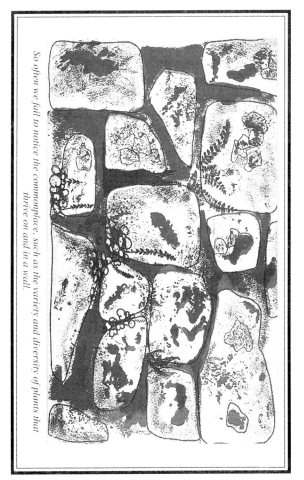

So often we fail to notice the commonplace, such as the variety and diversity of plants that thrive on and in a wall.

to escape along this road and was shot and died at this spot.

Just around the bends ahead, the fine sandstone buildings are the old coachouses and staff quarters of Brittas House.

Another 50m along the road, at another bend, there is a small lane to the right. Here, at the junction of this lane and the road, once stood the fine pillars and gates of the front entrance to the house.

The lane, which was created by the Land Commission to give access to farmers when the estate was divided, sweeps around to the side of the house, and runs through what were the terraced lawns on its northern side.

It is worth a short detour from our walk to see the ruins of the house and the remnants of the once magnificent gardens, which had many fine and exotic trees. In May and June the rich, red, rhododendrons are beautiful.

The castellated house was built in 1869 by General Francis Plunkett Dunne, to the design of architect John McCurdy, and stands on, or near, the previous ancestral home of the O'Dunnes, who were the chieftain rulers of the lands of Uí Riagáin, and descendants

Field Poppy *(Papaver rhoeas, family Papaveraceae)* The artillery
bombardments of the 1st. World War brought forth such a
profusion of red poppies on the battlefields, that the Poppy is the
symbol of that tragic time - 'Poppy Day'. Flowers May to August.

of the second century High King of Ireland, Cahir Mór. In 1622, when the earlier thatched castle and church stood here, the Tuath (territory) of Uí Riagáin was some 13,000 acres, with Brittas at its centre.

The Gothic style of architecture was the fashion in the early 1800's, and the house was no doubt a great improvement on the thatched mansion and church which it replaced. A new church was built in the village of Clonaslee in 1814. The inscription on the stone plaque over the door of the church reads:

"This church was erected with the consent of Charles Lindsey, Lord Bishop of Kildare, on a new site granted by Leiu. General Edward Dunne of Brittas. Consecrated on October 9, 1814."

Brittas House was burned down in 1942; some say it was arson, some an accident, all agree it was a tragedy.

Leaving the House, and back at the road/lane junction, continue along the road, over the culvert and turn left (west) into the forest plantation. Just here, in the depression on the left, now planted in spruce, was the garden of one of the two Dunne Sisters. Laid

BRITTAS HOUSE

Chinese Pagoda Plant
Introduced to Ireland as a food plant for Pheasants.

61

out in terraces, with a pond, and full of flowers, it was known as "Miss Kathleen's Garden". Some of the flowers still survive, now wild in the hedgerow.

Continue along this road through the plantation, for about 400m, to a fine stand of Scots Pine on the left. Just as you reach the grove of Scots Pine, pick your way through the young spruce plantation on the left, to the eastern end of the Artificial Lake. (Refer to Sketch Map). Here you will see the metal grille at the outflow, and be able to appreciate the care and skill with which this stone lined lake was made.

I believe that this lake was in fact the reservoir of water for Brittas House; water that was pumped up here by the hydraulic ram situated in the river, below the filter refered to earlier in this walk. It is interesting that the lake is only 20m above the river, and 10m above the level of Brittas House. The filter and ram are located at a point in the river nearest to the lake and house, and the lake is located in the nearest natural depression, at a suitable level and distance, above the house.

If this lake was to be no more than a

landscape ornament, then a far more suitable location for it would be in the depression in front of the entrance to the house, flooding "Miss Kathleen's Garden" and the hollow on the opposite side of the culvert.

__When leaving the lake, retrace your steps through the spruce to the forest road, and turn left.__

__After 200m (at the western end of the lake) the forest road turns northeast. Continue on the road and 200m farther on, where it forks, take the track to the right.__

As you walk this section, you will notice a plantation of Douglas Fir on your right. Their smooth, greyish bark appears to have small blisters. Burst one with your finger and smell the sap - no perfume or cologne could compete with the freshness of that scent !

__Keep left at the next junction, and just a 100m farther on, go straight through the crossroads.__

As you near the end of the plantation and come closer to the village you see, straight ahead of you, at the far end of the village, the church built by Col. Edward Dunne in 1814. This was the route taken from Brittas House

CHURCH OF IRELAND, CLONASLEE

when going to the Church on Sundays. As you pass through the gates on to "The Green", examine the finely crafted stonework of the gate piers, and indeed the small piers of the adjoining bungalow.

Just 30m beyond the gates you will pass, on your right, the old court house of Clonaslee. Practically all of the older houses in the village are built from local sandstone and it is a pity that such beauty should be hidden by a banal veneer of pebble dashing and plaster work.

On the left you will notice Hickeys; this building is approximately 300 years old and was always a public house. A good note on which to end this walk !

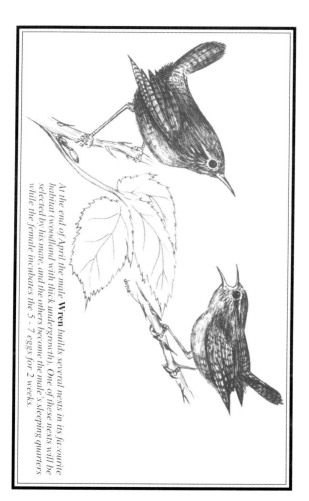

At the end of April the male **Wren** builds several nests in its favourite habitat (woodland with thick undergrowth). One of these nests will be selected by his mate, and the others become the male's sleeping quarters while the female incubates the 5 - 7 eggs for 2 weeks.

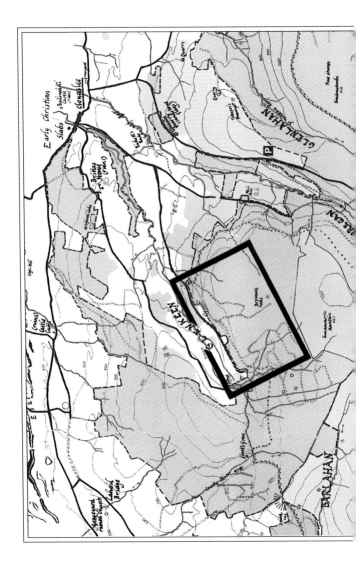

Walk 6
Brennan's Rocks - Glenkeen
6.5 km (4miles)

When I searched Slieve Bloom for a place to make my home, Glenkeen had a strong attraction which still remains. It is aptly named Gleann Caoin ("caoin" meaning gentle or mild) and its mildness appealed to many, because at one time it was the most populated glen in Slieve Bloom. In 1841 three hundred people lived in Glenkeen and as the raths and burial tumuli of the area testify, its history of occupation goes back to the earliest days.

To get to Glenkeen from the village of Clonaslee, take the road directly opposite the petrol pumps on the main street of the village, passing the water treatment plant (which supplies water to Tullamore) and following the line of the estate wall of Brittas Demesne.

After 1.6km (1 mile) at a junction, the road turns sharply to the right and winds its way along the southern side of the valley. Continue along this road for 2.5km (1.5 miles) and park 100m past the brown signpost for Glenkeen, at the entrance to the forest

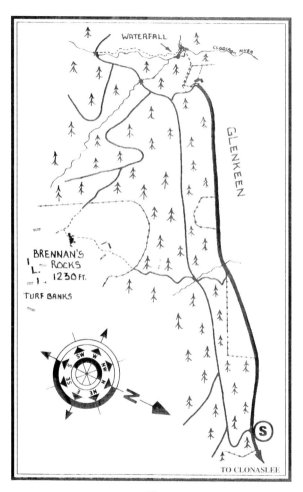

WATERFALL

CLODIAGH RIVER

GLENKEEN

BRENNAN'S
ROCKS
1230 FT.

TURF BANKS

N

S

TO CLONASLEE

plantation.

The walk begins on the forest road through the plantation; continuing on an old cart track to the turf banks on the high moorland; descending from Brennan's Rocks through forestry; to the quarry pits and waterfall on the river Clodiagh at the head of the valley and returns to the start on the county road.

From the entrance to the plantation the gravel road curves through Larch and Lodgepole to the first junction. Keep right at this, and the next forest road junction, 300m farther on. Because of its high resistance to weathering and decay, Larch has been traditionally used in the building of the '18 Foot' lake boat, as well as 'bog barrows' and the now almost forgotten horse's cart.

After another 500m, at a small stream and lay-by, a rough track rises from the right and continues into the trees on the left. Follow this track to the left, ascending through the trees. The track is deeply cut and strewn with rounded quartz pebbles, which provide a geological clue to the structure of the mountains. The quartz pebbles, which are extremely hard, were rolled and rounded in the bed of a huge river which flowed over this landscape almost 400 million years ago. Eventually, as layer upon layer of various materials were laid on top, these pebbles, and the river sand in which they lay, were cemented together, into a kind of natural concrete called conglomerate rock. With the passing of time this rock became exposed and with the action of rain, wind, and frost was again reduced to sand and pebbles.

Generations of inhabitants in Glenkeen drew turf from the mountain bog along this track using sleighs, rather than carts - the sleighs sliding over the uneven soft ground, where cart wheels would sink.

As the track continues through the trees, its surface, in places, deteriorates to moss covered, waterlogged peat. Near the end of the forest plantation, an older branch of the track runs off to the right, keep to the left and continue to the end of the plantation.

Stay on the track out onto the mountain bog, heading due south, towards the higher ground of the knoll to the right.

The heather is knee deep in places, and

the track eventually fades into the landscape, marked only by the occasional pile of lichen covered, sandstone and conglomerate rocks.

As you ***ascend the higher ground to the south,*** the view back over Glenkeen, and the flat land to the north, is expansive. In the distance, overlooking forest covered Barradoo, you can see (to the northwest) the cooling towers of the ESB power station at Lumcloon (near Ferbane) 21km (13 miles) away; to the north, Tullamore, and to the northeast, Croghan Hill and the towers of Rhode power station 38km (23 miles) away. From the top of this hill, looking south over the saddle to the humpback of Knockachorra, and southwest to the communications masts on top of Wolftrap, the extent of generations of turfcutting is evident in the network of heather cloaked turfbanks all around.

Contour around to the southern side of the knoll to find the heather covered sandstone and conglomerate outcrop that is "Brennan's Rocks" - a place where I, and I'm sure hundreds of turf cutters before me, sat to eat and rest. At a height of 380m (1250 feet) this can be a windswept and miserable place in bad weather, but in sunshine you could stay here for hours.

__From the rocks, descend to the southwest towards the masts on Wolftrap, to meet a track which leads from the turf banks into the forest plantation. At the track turn right.__

Soon after the track enters the plantation you will notice underfoot and in the bank on the right, an exposure of crimson coloured soil. This is silt, laid down on the floodplain of the same huge river that flowed here 400 million years ago, and laid down the eroded quartz pebbles which are scattered all around. At that time the continent of which Ireland was a part, lay roughly where West Africa is now. When the river floods receded, the silt oxidised to a red color, burned by the scorching equatorial sun. 100 million years later, as that continent drifted to these northern latitudes, its landscape was folded, leaving these river deposits at this level.

As you descend, on the left, in the shade of the trees, are wonderful carpets of sphagnum, and small, conical clumps of polytrichum.

At the junction with the next forest road, turn right, and continue descending through the plantation to the next forest road junction, where you turn left.

After 50m the road crosses a stream and rises to another bend. Continue along this road, past a forest road junction, to the concrete ford at the next stream.

At this ford, in the sandstone bedrock of the river, can be seen three boreholes, evidence of past quarrying. *Cross the ford, and immediately turn right, leaving the road to descend through the trees, on the west bank of the river. As you make your way downstream through the trees, watch carefully for the clear route of the deer path, which runs close to the river and leads you to the waterfall.*

Follow the deer path past the waterfall to a deep gully, and descend the gully to the river. At the river and just to the right, on the opposite bank, is an abandoned Slieve Bloom Way marker, its yellow arrow conveniently pointing in the direction you must take when leaving this place.

The waterfall, unlike that in Glenbarrow,

is manmade, resulting from the quarrying of the riverbed sandstone. Before the advent of cement, stone was used for building walls, windowsills, lintels and floors, and also for gate piers, and fine examples of its use will be seen later, on the road back to the start.

When leaving the waterfall, retrace your steps to the Slieve Bloom Way marker, and with your back to the river, ascend the forest ride immediately to the left of the old quarry face and depression.

At the top of the ride line, at the edge of the plantation, turn right along the cleared pathway. At the end of this pathway, where a wide ride line runs off to the right, cross the earthbank and continue on to meet a rough lane, some 20m away.

Turn left at the lane and descend to the farm. Here a Slieve Bloom Way marker directs you past the farm, along the road and back to the start.

As you walk along the road, you will see on the left, very fine examples of the cratfsmanship with which some of the gate piers were made. The first such pair you meet are dated 1896, others are more ornate, some

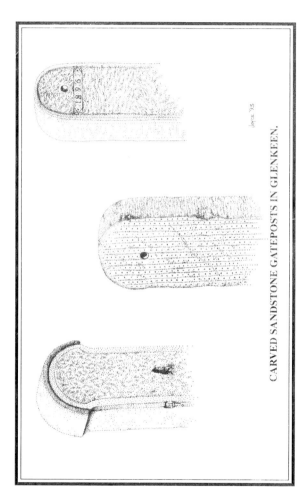

CARVED SANDSTONE GATEPOSTS IN GLENKEEN.

extremely rough, like megalithic standing stones.

It's a pleasant walk back to the start, 1.6km (1 mile) away, with fine views of the valley and beyond.

Walk 7
Glendineoregan Waterfall
4.8km (3miles)

At the head of Glendineoregan, or Glendine as it is known locally, is a forgotten waterfall, hidden away among the trees. It is not the biggest, tallest or widest in the mountains, in fact it falls about 10m and is usually about 1m wide, (although it can be as much as 7m wide at times of heavy rainfall). But what makes it attractive is its vertical fall, and its setting among ash and willow, with the coniferous backdrop.

In 1992, much of the valley was clearfelled, and heavy machinery cut a new track on the eastern side of the river, making the approach to the waterfall much easier than before.

To get to the start from the village of Clonaslee, follow signposts for 'Mountain Drive' and 'The Cut'.

Begin at The Cut, and I suggest that

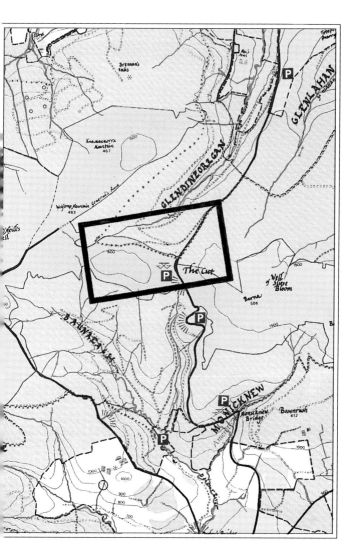

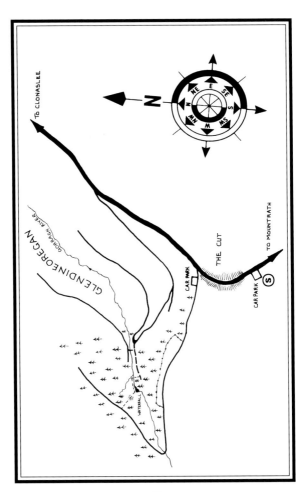

To CLONASLEE

GLENDINEOREGAN

BORRAGH RIVER

WATERFALL

CAR PARK

THE CUT

CAR PARK

To MOUNTRATH

S

N

NE E SE

N S

NW SW

W SW

you park on the southern side, rather than the northern side, so that you have to walk through the Cut and see it more closely.

This road over the mountain probably comes close to the line of a much more ancient route to the north. The summit to the east of The Cut is called Barna, meaning 'gap' or 'pass' in Irish.

Near the northern end of The Cut, high up on the right (eastern side) are the initials of two workmen who cut this pass through the rock in the 1840's. The quality of the carving indicates that they were both accomplished stonemasons and it is interesting that they carefully carved out the full name of their townlands : proud of their work and advertising their skill. I feel sure that at that time, 'DJ' of Killinure and 'MC' of Curragh were well known craftsmen.

Continue past the northern car park and along the county road towards Clonaslee.

Avoid the temptation to descend directly from the northern car park to the forest road in the valley floor; the ground is extremely rough, and you could easily twist an ankle

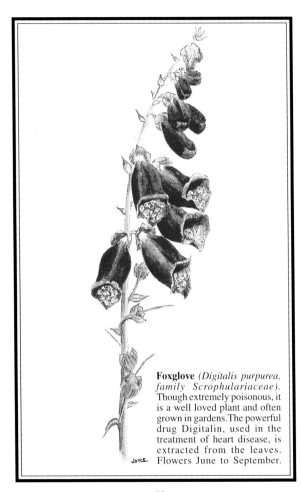

Foxglove *(Digitalis purpurea, family Scrophulariaceae).* Though extremely poisonous, it is a well loved plant and often grown in gardens. The powerful drug Digitalin, used in the treatment of heart disease, is extracted from the leaves. Flowers June to September.

Joyce.

among the tree stumps and branches hidden by the sedges and grasses.

A few hundred yards along the road, on the left, at the roadside, you will see an iron cross, erected to the memory of Michael Delaney, a forest worker like his father before him, who died at work near this spot, on the morning of 18th. September 1975. His was 'the last house' in the valley of Glendineoregan and it now stands idle.

Continue along the road for another 200m and turn left, heading southwest, on to the forest road that descends to the Gorragh River in the floor of the valley. You will appreciate the steep sided, bowl shape, which gives this valley its name - Glendine (Gleann Doighin) meaning 'deep glen'.

With the felling of the trees in Glendineoregan; the development of the plantations in Glenlahan and Cones; and the open range of the moorland, this valley has become one of the hunting grounds of Slieve Bloom's largest bird of prey, the Hen Harrier. With a wingspan of over 1m, they can be seen quartering the area in the summer months as they search for fieldmice, shrews and other small mammals. The female is brown; the male a greyish blue colour, with a wingspan slightly smaller than the female. A more frequent sight is the Kestrel, hovering, then gliding away to hover again nearby.

If you descend this track in late Autumn, when the grasses are dying back, it is easy to appreciate the ancestry of our present day wheat, barley and oats, all of which have been bred from wild grasses similar to these.

At the bottom of the valley, near the stream, the forest road turns sharply to the right. Do not cross the stream, but go to the left, on a rough track, which runs parallel to the stream, and steadily ascends towards the trees at the top of the river valley. Continue on this track as far as the mature trees, then descend to the stream junction on your right. It is best to cross the stream at this point, and continue with care, on the opposite bank, to the waterfall, just 50m above.

On almost every occasion that I have come to this waterfall I have seen the wild goats that inhabit Slieve Bloom. They are impressive animals, particularly the adult

KESTREL ON A PLUCKING POST

males with their long, backward curving horns and shaggy beards. Their colour varies from all white, to almost all black, with combinations of black, brown and white. The darker coloured animals blend perfectly with the landscape, and can be hard to spot, but the white ones are very obvious. Watch for their prints, which are similar to the fallow deer, but the cleaves are more open.

In the 1700's the keeping of goats was discouraged, to the extent that a fine of '20 shillings' (£1) per goat was imposed on anyone who kept one. In the 1800's some landlords threatened a fine of £5 per goat on their tenants. The result of this penal 'tax' on what was the main source of meat and milk, was a dramatic increase in the "wild" goat population - an inventive, and typically Irish, solution to the problem.

Today these feral goats have a special place in the ecosystem of Slieve Bloom, and add much to the charm of the mountains.

__When leaving the waterfall, head northwest into a depression caused by a recent landslide. Ascend to the back of this depression, and continue ascending, on very__

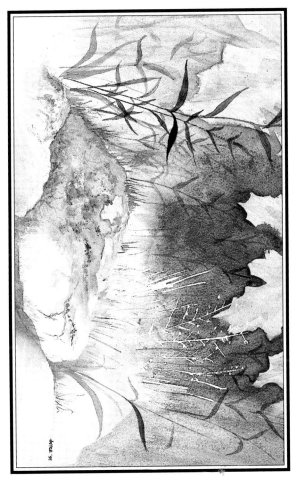

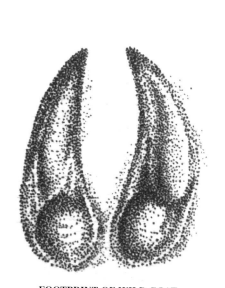

FOOTPRINT OF WILD GOAT
The shape and open cleave makes the feral goat print easily distinguishable from the deer.

steep ground covered with woodrush, northwest, as high as you can, before you are forced to enter the trees. Pick your way on a 'brashed' track through the trees, to the forest road, 100m away. At the road turn left.

The road winds its way around the top of Glendineoregan, first to the southwest, then to the east, and back to the northern car park at The Cut. Along the way there are good exposures of the blanket peat and many interesting, but often unnoticed plants, particularly the beautifully coloured lichens.

Walk 8
Cumber Hillfort - 4km (2.5 miles)

Northwestern Slieve Bloom, in the vicinity of Kinnitty, has a history of occupation and settlement stretching back at least 4000 years.

The ringfort on the summit of Cumber Hill is one of a number of earthworks and standing stones which, at first sight, might seem randomly scattered over the landscape of Forelacka and Cumber. However, their locations are far from random, and closer examination shows evidence of very careful positioning.

The hillfort on Cumber is, I believe, one of at least eight, which were strategically placed to give commanding views of the area.

The ringforts on Cumber Hill; the summit of Knocknaman; the southwest shoulder of Broom Hill (east of Cumber Hill); are triangulated, so that the blind spots of one can be seen by another. Five other ringforts, immediately outside this triangle, complete

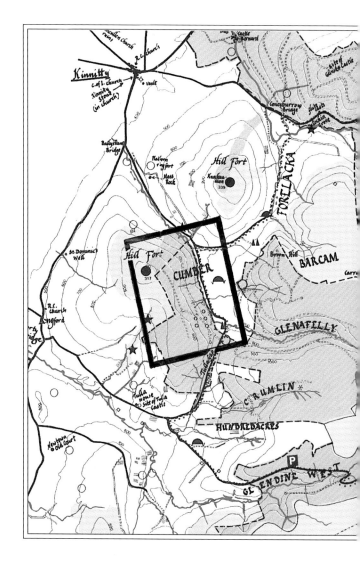

the pattern; and all together, give total control of this major thoroughfare through Slieve Bloom.

The major thoroughfare I refer to is the Slí Dághla, or the Munster Road, one of the 'Five Great Roads' that radiated from Tara, about 2000 yrs. ago.

The traditional route of this slí is along the Camcor River, past Castle Bernard, Coneyburrow Bridge, into Forelacka, Cumber and on through the Tulla Gap. A 'branch road' ran northwest, through the Cumber valley, past Knocknaman's southwestern slopes.

The slí made use of much earlier routes through the mountains, and without doubt, settlement in the Cumber valley predates the Slí Dághla, by at least a thousand years.

To get to the start from the village of Kinnitty, take the road for Roscrea. After 1.6km (1 mile) turn left at Ballyshane Bridge, signposted for the Slieve Bloom Way and the Old Munster Road.

After 2.4km (1.5 miles) at a fork in the road (where the Slieve Bloom Way and the Old Munster Road are signposted to the left), keep right. Almost 1km (0.6 miles) farther on,

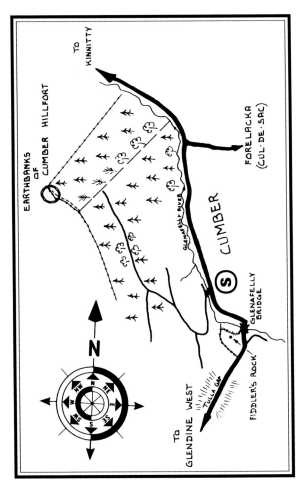

TO
KINNITTY

EARTHBANKS
OF
CUMBER HILLFORT

FORELACKA
(CUL-DE-SAC)

GLENAFELLY RIVER

S CUMBER

GLENAFELLY
BRIDGE

TULLA GAP

FIDDLER'S ROCK

TO
GLENDINE WEST

N

NW N NE
W   E
SW S SE

you come to a forest entrance on the right. Park here.

To start the walk, cross the concrete bridge over the Glenafelly River, and ascend the forest road to the left.

At the bend in the road, look East towards the valley of Glenafelly. Immediately below you, in a field beside the river, stands a large block of quartzite, known as the Fiddler's Rock.

Quartzite does not occur naturally in Slieve Bloom. This rock is a glacial erratic, carried here by the ice sheets of 15,000 years ago. Quartzite is very rarely found in the glacial deposits and this, the largest block of quartzite in the whole of Slieve Bloom, may have been deliberately brought here to mark this location.

It is believed that quartzite had a special ritual or magical significance to the early Bronze Age people, and quartzite rocks like these were erected to mark specially significant locations.

There is little doubt that this rock served such a purpose. It is aligned with the entrance stone of a Bronze Age passage grave 2000m away and some 200m from the passage grave stand two grotesquely weathered pillars of limestone, about seven feet apart. A line from the Fiddler's Rock to the entrance stone of the passage grave passes between, and at right angles to, these weathered limestone pillars.

The summit of Knocknaman (which itself may have had a spiritual and ritual significance, because of the strangely fire-marked stones found there) lies exactly to the North of the Fiddler's Rock.

Keep right at the junction just 20m past the bend and left at the next junction, 200m farther on.

As you ascend to the spruce trees ahead there is a wonderful view over the whole area.

At the next junction, among the trees, take the road to the right, heading northwest.

Along this road is a very pleasant plantation of beech, which relieves the monotony of the spruce. ***Continue along this road through the spruce to a wide ride line planted with birch. Turn left, due southwest, uphill, along the ride line.***

Though the ground is rough and littered

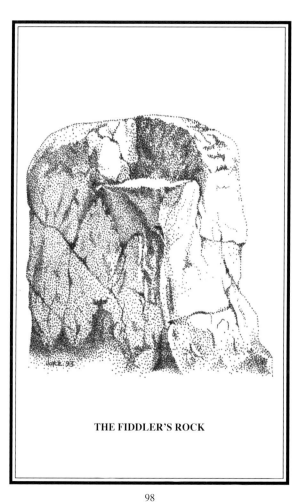

THE FIDDLER'S ROCK

with branches from the thinning of the plantation, you will have little difficulty finding a deer path.

__When you reach the end of the ride line turn right (northwest) into the forest plantation of Noble Fir. Continue through the trees (keeping near to, and parallel with, the forest boundary) to the open ground and ringfort on the summit of Cumber Hill.__ Follow the circular earthbanks to the northwestern side of the ringfort where your efforts will be richly rewarded with the most spectacular panorama of the surrounding countryside.

__When leaving the ringfort it is best to retrace your route through the Noble Fir to the ride line. Descend along the ride line, due northwest, past the junction with the forest road.__

Below the junction the birch gives way to a lovely plantation of beech and with luck you might see the fallow deer who frequent this area. This section through the beech is quite steep and in autumn and winter the fallen leaves can be very slippery underfoot.

FALLOW DEER IN SUMMER

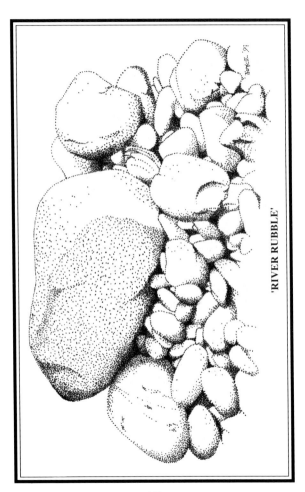

'RIVER RUBBLE'

__Continue descending along the ride line through the beech wood to the hazel scrub beside the river. Pick your way through the scrub to the river and head southeast, upstream.__

If the water level is low you might find the easiest route is along the gravel margin of the riverbed and though the river bends and meanders, and you will end up with wet boots, it is a most pleasant and enjoyable walk. *__The other option is to cross the stream and go directly through the wood to the road beyond. At the road turn right (southeast) back to the start.__*

In the river, among the river gravels, you will notice lots of limestone that has been washed down from the glacial drift in Glenafelly. At a particular place the river has cut through the putty like grey deposits of what was once the bottom of a lake filled with the cold water of the melting ice.

The strip of woodland by the river, where birch, ash, hazel and beech grow alongside the conifers, is home to a great variety of plants and animals and in the soft,

Friend of the Oak', the **Jay** is most abundant in oak woods. In April or May it builds its nest about 15 feet from the ground in the dense branches of spruce, usually on the margins of a wood.

damp places, you will find prints of deer, badger, fox and mink. This woodland is also ideal territory for the jay. Its call (a penetrating 'skraak') is unmistakable. It is a very wary, cautious bird and if you hear its call the chances are that you won't see it.

A member of the crow family (like the magpie) this beautiful bird was once classed as vermin and was mercilessly hunted, its beautiful blue-flashed wings being the prize. But jays play a crucial role in the spread of oak woods.

In the autumn when voles, squirrels and woodmice are hoarding acorns for the winter, they deliberately nip the acorn's sprouting tip to prevent germination. On the other hand jays collect healthy, undamaged acorns, directly from the trees, and bury them in open spaces at a depth ideal for germination. When these larders are forgotten, the oak gets a chance to reproduce. In fact the oak's chances of reproduction depend so exclusively on the jay that it designs and grows its acorns to be stolen by jays and those not stolen are, quite literally, surplus to requirements.

As you continue upstream the road on

the left comes, in places, to within 10m of the stream, so at any stage you may choose to end your river walk and continue on the road. If you stay with the river you eventually arrive at the start - the concrete bridge at the forest entrance.

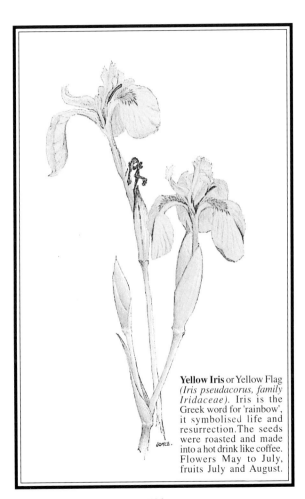

Yellow Iris or Yellow Flag
*(Iris pseudacorus, family
Iridaceae).* Iris is the
Greek word for 'rainbow',
it symbolised life and
resurrection. The seeds
were roasted and made
into a hot drink like coffee.
Flowers May to July,
fruits July and August.

JOYCE.

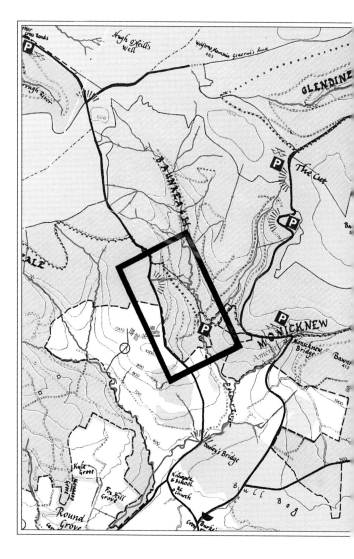

Walk 9
Baunreagh - Castleconnor
4km (2.5 miles)

Baunreagh is one of those valley through which people drive and see only trees, but for the inquisitive walker there are signs and traces of a fascinating past.

To get to the start; from Kinnitty take the road for Mountrath (signposted Mountrath 23km) and follow signposts for the Delour Valley and Baunreagh; from Clonaslee take The Cut road and 3km (almost 2 miles) beyond The Cut, turn right into the forest plantation (signposted Baunreagh); from Mountrath follow signposts for Kinnitty and the Delour Valley.

Whether you approach Baunreagh from Clonaslee, Mountrath or Kinnitty, it will be necessary to drive through the forest to reach the car park in the valley.

The buildings adjacent to the car park are all that remain of Baunreagh House, which was demolished in the 1960's. The house stood where the car park is now, and the

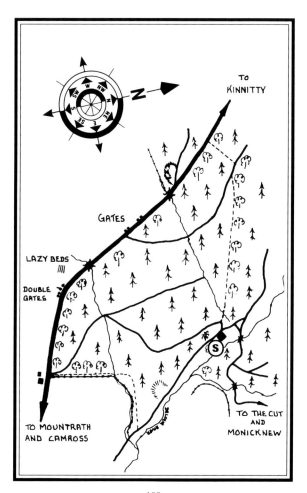

TO
KINNITTY

GATES

LAZY BEDS

DOUBLE
GATES

S

TO MOUNTRATH
AND CAMROSS

TO THE CUT
AND
MONICKNEW

adjacent buildings were retained for the storage of forestry equipment.

The Monkey Puzzle tree *(Araucaria araucana)* opposite the car park, is a native of Chile, and would have been planted as an ornamental lawn tree. The *Berberis Darwinii* (among the rhododendrons to the right of the Monkey Puzzle, and now 3m high) date from the same time and would have been modest garden shrubs when the house was in its prime. In the area around the car park you will find laurel, rhododendron, and other trees and shrubs that were associated with the house.

__Leaving the car park, turn left at the fork in the road, opposite the gates to the buildings.__

__The road continues uphill and, after only a short distance, swings to the left. Keep right (northwest) and follow a rough track, indicated by a Slieve Bloom Way marker, uphill through coniferous trees that give way to beech and continue to the forest road above.__

As you ascend the track notice, on the left, the mosses hanging from the trees and carpeting the ground, giving an athmosphere of tropical rainforest. Among the moss grows the delicate Wood Sorrel, also called Cuckoo's Meat and Wild Shamrock. Indeed it is most probable that if Saint Patrick used a plant to explain his teachings, he would have chosen the Wood Sorrel rather than the Shamrock, as this medicinal plant would have been well known as an aid to digestion and as a poultice to reduce inflammation. To-day it is often used in small quantities in salads and soups. The red veined, white flowers appear from about March to July.

__Keep to the right at the forest road and after 30m, opposite a turning marker for the Slieve Bloom Way, ascend the bank on the left and make your way uphill through larch and spruce to a beech plantation at the county road.__

__At the county road turn left.__ As you head downhill, on the right, you will notice an old 'slig' quarry. This material is a siltstone, often referred to locally as 'gritstone' or 'slig', and like the finer grained mudrock at the waterfall in Glenbarrow, and the loose siltstone in the forest below Brennan's Rocks, was oxidised to this red colour by the blazing equatorial sun, which shone on this part of the world (when it lay near the equator) 400 million years ago. Because 'slig' compacts so well, it made an excellent filling for the road surfaces in the forest plantations of Baunreagh and Gorteenameale. Farther into the pit the undisturbed loose stone is covered in a lichen called Lecidea, which employs a kind of chemical warfare to protect its boundary with neighbouring lichens. On closer examination the boundaries are visible as black lines between each individual plant.

It is interesting to see how the seeds of the surrounding trees (soon to be felled) have seeded so naturally and so well in this seemingly inhospitable, but sheltered, pit.

Just about 40m further down the road is an easily missed culvert with a wonderfully constructed bridge. Its construction can only be fully appreciated by descending into the gully on the left. The spruce tree, which was so carelessly planted beside the bridge, on the slope of the gully, has, in its search for support and food, extended its roots above ground, to the extent that one has grown along the ledge of the bridge, crossing the stream, to root on the other side of the gully.

This bridge dates from the mid 1700's when a turnpike (or toll road) was constructed over the mountains from Mountrath to Lackaroe crossroads and on to Kilcormac and Birr. The bridges cost, at that time, £10 each and it is a credit to the quality of the workmanship that they are still in such fine repair.

As you continue downhill along the road you will see on the right some fine stonework in the gateposts and stile at a field entrance. The capstone on the left, at the stile, is initialed 'PM' and dated 1908. A few metres further on, another set of gate piers and stile display the same craft and skill with stone.

At the bottom of the hill, past the next culvert, is a double set of gates on the right. Here, behind the left hand gate, is a most impressive sandstone structure built to cover and protect a spring well. The water flows from beneath the curving wall through two metal-grilled holes into a shallow trough and overflows into a channel carved in sandstone flags. Perhaps this was a place to water the coach horses after the first part of their climb

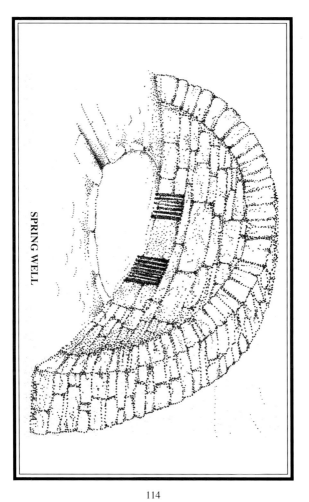

SPRING WELL

over the mountains.

At these double gates, if you look due northwest into the field, you will see the lazy beds in which the potatoes rotted in the Great Famine of 1846. The only contemporary account of the catastrophic failure of the potato crop was written by a man who resided at Cardtown House (about 3km to the southwest).

This man, William Stuart Trench, had spent many years experimenting with the reclamation of the heather covered mountain land of this very valley, Baunreagh. His system was to plough the heather and spread about 7500 litres (1600 gallons) of lime to the acre, dig trenches, and mound the heather and soil into 1.5m wide lazy beds. The potatoes were then planted in these beds. Guano, the dried bird manure imported from coastal South America, was then spread on the lazy beds, and finally the guano was topped with more soil from the trenches on either side.

Trench's reclamation experiments succeeded beyond even his wildest expectations, and the land so improved, that he could even grow corn crops.

For many years previous to 1846, he employed over 200 full time labourers, who worked at draining, levelling, the production of lime, planting and digging etc. These efforts at reclamation in Baunreagh had come to the attention of many of Ireland's leading agriculturalists, to such an extent that Stuart Trench was awarded the Silver and Gold Medals of the Royal Agricultural Society of Ireland.

In 1846 he had 162 acres under potatoes and by July his crop was in marvelous condition. On the 1st. August he heard rumours of this new disease in the district. He rode to Baunreagh, but all seemed well. He rode to the reported locations of the blight in the lowlands and saw the withered potato stalks and smelt the horrible stink hanging over the potato fields.

On each of the next four days he checked his crop in Baunreagh; all seemed well and the stalks were luxuriant and healthy. On the 6th. of August, as he rode up the valley he knew, by the horrible smell rising from the fields, that his crop, though apparently healthy, was rotting in the ground.

Because of the number employed, the good wages they earned and the abundant produce, Baunreagh was known as the 'Happy Valley', but it all ended suddenly, on the 6th. of August 1846.

William Stuart Trench had spent £10,000 for his land, £8,000 for buildings, drainage and reclamation, and lost £3,000 on his crop. (See "Realities of Irish Life" by W. Stuart Trench, 1868, abridged edition by Macgibbon & Kee 1966).

__Continue on the road (or enter the beech wood on the left and walk parallel to the road) until you come to the forest entrance opposite the farm yard. This forest road leads through the plantation to the buildings at the car park. However, a more interesting and pleasant route is to descend through the mature beech at the edge of the coniferous plantation, enjoying the wonderful view over the Delour Valley.__

As you descend you will notice the hawthorn ditch on the right with its even spacing and layering (i.e. half cutting the branches and laying them horizontally, to

Wind of Change in Baunreagh

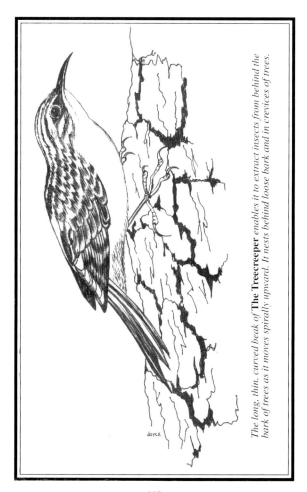

The long, thin, curved beak of **The Treecreeper** enables it to extract insects from behind the bark of trees as it moves spirally upward. It nests behind loose bark and in crevices of trees.

JOYCE.

thicken the ditch and close the spaces
between the individual trees). Hawthorn
ditches were grown by placing the ripe haws
in a straw rope, which was then dipped in a
solution of urine and rainwater, and placed
along the line of the required ditch. A shallow
trench was dug beside the rope and the rope
buried. The urine had the effect of
decomposing the straw to a compost which
fertilised the young seedlings.

*At the end of this beech ride you should
cross the stream gully and continue along
by the fence.* Where the fence turns away from
the stream there is a badger's sett on the right,
under the fence.

*At the open ground, where the fence
turns sharply to the right (east), leave the
fence, and avoiding the area of brambles,
woodrush and holly, ascend through the
young beech trees to the coniferous trees on
the higher ground ahead.*

*At the conifers turn right and continue
parallel to an old earthbank.*

*At the end of the earthbank keep to the
right and continuing through the woodrush
keep the last of the young beech on your left.*

__Soon you will come to a cleared area above the forest road,__ overlooking Monicknew (Móin 'ic Nuadha - Mc Noone's Bog) to the east, and Inchanisky (Inis an Esc - The Low Meadow at the Track by the Stream). *__Carefully descend over rough ground littered with branches, brambles and holly, to the forest road below. At the road turn left.__*

A short distance along this road, on the right, is a stone erected to the memory of John Carroll, Killinure, who died here on the 16th. February 1956 aged 22 years.

On a dark, wet, February evening, John was cycling home from work in the forest plantation when he was struck by the trailer of a lorry and suffered severe head injuries. His two brothers and workmates carried him back to Baunreagh House, but he was already dead.

__Continue along the road to the car park. However, if you are prepared to get your feet wet, a more interesting route back to the car park is by the river ; either on the bank, or in the stream itself. At the confluence of the streams (see sketch map)__

Holly (*Ilex acquifolium, family Acquifoliaceae*).
A mystical tree of winter. Even before Christian times it was
believed that the sprays of red holly berries protected the
house against evil. Holly trees were planted near houses
to ward off lightning.

Holly is a poisonous plant, likes a moist rather acid soil and is
sensitive to frost. Flowers May to August,
fruits September to March.

The Pine Marten is the 'cat' referred to in many ancient Irish manuscripts, and is Ireland's rarest mammal, having been hunted almost to extinction. Happily this shy, elusive creature is making a comeback in Slieve Bloom.

follow the left hand tributary to the concrete bridge just beyond the car park buildings. (The right hand tributary meets the same forest road at a similar concrete bridge further away from the car park).

At the bridge turn left, and continue along the forest road back to the car park.

Walk 10
Glendine - Arderin - Glenamoon
9km (5.5 miles)

The name 'Arderin', meaning 'The Height of Ireland', appears in the *Inquisito Lageniae* (Inquisition of Leinster) dated 1621, and presumably the name was in use long before that. Though only 527m (1735 feet) high, the summit of Arderin provides a magnificent view of the country.

Writing in 1819, J.Baldwin reports : *"The view from 'The Height of Ireland' comprises 15 counties, and is perhaps the most extensive and richest in Ireland".*

T.L. Cooke, in 1875, remarked that the view is *"bounded almost solely by the powers of vision".*

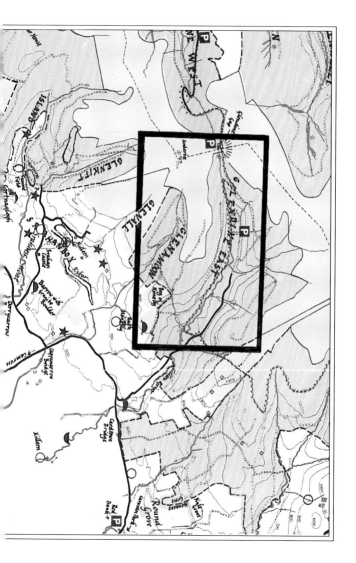

To get to Glendine East refer to the Slieve Bloom Environment Park Map.

In the autumn of 1994 Laois County Council completed the eastern section of the road through the Gap of Glendine. At the time of writing, it is best to drive into Glendine East from the county road at Cardtown Bridge.

After 2km (1.25 miles) turn left at the Slieve Bloom Way marker.

As you near the start of the walk, on the left, you will notice an unusual, flat topped, circular mound rising perhaps 10m above the river bed, and over 60m in diameter. This mound of glacial debris was probably the end moraine of the southeastward flowing glacier that carved out Glendine 15,000 years ago.

However, could its present shape have been moulded by the hand of man, perhaps for a ritual purpose associated with the pagan festival of Lughnasa, which was celebrated in this valley and on the slopes of Arderin? Or perhaps the site of a ring fort? The commanding view from the top of the mound suggests that it would have been an ideal location for a ring fort.

GLENDALE AFTER THE ICE

JOYCE '91

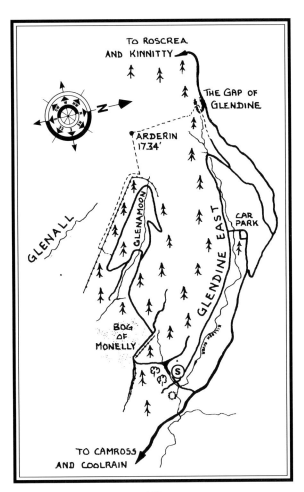

TO ROSCREA
AND KINNITTY

THE GAP OF
GLENDINE

ARDERIN
17.34'

GLENALL

GLENAMOON

GLENDINE EAST

CAR
PARK

BOG
OF
MONELLY

S

TO CAMROSS
AND COOLRAIN

129

In time it will be hidden as the mound and the surrounding land is now planted in Beech and Ash.

Begin your walk at the mouth of Glendine East, parking at the junction of the 4 forest roads, just past the concrete bridge over the Killeen river, at the brown signpost for Glenamoon.

From the start, follow the tarred road northwest into the valley of Glendine (Gleann Doighin - The Deep Glen).

After 2km (1.25 miles) at the stand of mature spruce trees, a forest road branches off to the right to a cleared, green picnic area among the trees.

Keep to the left, following the Slieve Bloom Way marker, rising uphill, due west, past an old 'gritstone' quarry.

At the confluence of the headwaters of the Killeen river, where the two streams fall in small but delightful cascades, the road turns sharply to the right and continues on the northern side of the valley.

About 100m farther on, a rough track branches off to the left, ignore this track and continue for another 200m to a junction.

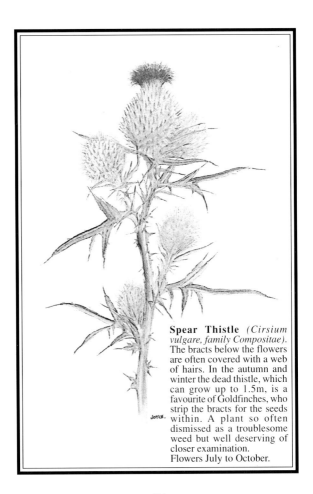

Spear Thistle (*Cirsium vulgare, family Compositae*). The bracts below the flowers are often covered with a web of hairs. In the autumn and winter the dead thistle, which can grow up to 1.5m, is a favourite of Goldfinches, who strip the bracts for the seeds within. A plant so often dismissed as a troublesome weed but well deserving of closer examination.
Flowers July to October.

Turn left, ascending due west, towards the Gap of Glendine. In 1993 the upper reaches of Glendine East were clearfelled, and in places, the tangle of branches, tree trunks and material washed down from the earthworks associated with the new road, can be an awkward obstacle to overcome.

As you near the Gap, the stream gully divides, and though the branch to the left looks inviting, it will lead you astray. Keep to the right, ascending on a path over rough, often wet ground, through the trees to the open ground at the Gap. As you walk, listen for the deep, repeated 'prruk' of the ravens that inhabit the upper reaches of the valley.

This pass, linking Laois and Offaly through the Gap of Glendine, is a very ancient and much travelled route. It appears to have been a slí, which branched off from the Slí Dághla south of the Tulla Gap (see Walk 8) crossing the mountain through the Gap of Glendine to join the other major routes, or slighs, on the eastern side of Slieve Bloom.

It is said that Saint Patrick rested at the Gap as he journeyed from Offaly into Laois; it appears in a Map of Ireland by the famous

Flemish geographer Gerardus Mercator (1512 - 1594); in the 1700's it was the most important route through the mountains, and in 1801, Charles Coote describes the route through the Gap as being *"very difficult of approach, steep and craggy, and not five feet wide"*.

In the Gap there once grew a hawthorn tree, known as The Criochan Thorn. It was one of twelve sacred thorn bushes documented for the province of Leinster. Of the twelve, three are in the Slieve Bloom area : The Criochan Thorn, in the Gap of Glendine, Saint Kieran's Thorn, at Saighir, southwest of Kinnitty on the road to Roscrea and The Monument Bush in Camross.

In pre Christian times the pagan Celtic Festival of Lughnasa was celebrated in early August on the slopes of Arderin and at the Criochan Thorn in the Gap. The first corn of the harvest was cut, and these first fruits of the harvest were carried up the mountain and offered to the God of the Harvest. Then the festivities began with the eating of the bilberries, or 'fraocháin' as they are known in Irish.

Hawthorn *(Crataegus monogyna, family Rosaceae).*
Also known as the May Bush or Whitethorn, it likes a shallow,
stoney soil and withstands drought.

The Maybush signified the oncoming spring, the end of winter
and the rebirth of life. It is considered very unlucky to cut down
a Hawthorn. Flowers May to June. Fruits August to November.

This pagan festival was later Christianised and the celebrations of the first fruits of the harvest became Height Sunday, or Fraochán Sunday, and the date changed from August to the last Sunday in July. The celebration of Fraochán Sunday in Glendine was known as 'The Pattern of the Gap' and was famous all over central Ireland.

At the Gap continue for 20m past the Slieve Bloom Way marker on the left and ascend, on a rough track through the heather, due southeast, towards the open moorland.

After about 200m, this rough track turns to the east. At this point leave the track and head due south through the heather towards the summit of Arderin. This is a wild and open landscape, and because of its height, often cloaked in mist and cloud. Even in good visibility check your compass often and maintain your direction due south. Because of Arderin's even, domed shape, as you climb, through the often knee deep heather, observe the outline of the mountain against the sky; always heading towards the top of the dome.

The summit is marked by a small cairn of turf sods beside the small, concrete slab of the Ordnance Survey triangulation platform. Close by, some masts (with their accompanying wind generators and shed) have mushroomed, and perhaps like mushrooms they will fade away in time.

__When leaving the summit head due east across the heather, towards the valley of Glenamoon.__ The name Glenamoon is most probably derived from the Irish, 'gleann'- glen and 'móin' - turf, and was known locally as Gleann na Móna - The Glen of the Turf (though in Daniel Cahill's Grand Jury Maps of 1805, it appears as Gleann Mín - The Smooth Glen).

__As you reach the trees at the head of Glenamoon you will come to a wet track through the blanket bog. This track encircles the head of the valley. Follow this track to the right and descend along the edge of the forest plantation on your left, heading southeast.__

As you descend there is a fine view of the flat land to the south of Portlaoise, and to the right, the eskers and glacial deposits in

DROPPINGS OF DEER, HARE AND RABBIT

Deer

Hare

Rabbit

Srahanboy and at the mouth of Glenall valley.

At the end of the mature forest, where it gives way to a much younger plantation, leave the track, and turning left, cross the fence. Make your way northeast, between the young spruce, keeping parallel to the mature pine on the left.

Watch for the deer paths (often littered with droppings) between the young trees. Though the paths meander, they provide a sure footed route to the forest road, 100m ahead.

At the forest road turn right and continue downhill round the bend. Keep left at the next junction.

At the next bend the road crosses a small stream and begins to ascend towards the east, out of the valley. Keep right at the forest road junction just ahead.

As you ascend and leave Glenamoon, look back to appreciate the lovely shape of this half forgotten valley.

After about 1.6km (1 mile) on the left, a rough track meets the road. This track, which winds its way through the spruce plantation to the blanket bog, was a route to the turf banks on the ridge between Glenamoon and Glendine East.

__Continue on the forest road, which turns sharply to the right, skirting the edge of the mature coniferous plantation.__ Behind the bank on the right is the Bog of Monelly where in the 1650's the dispossessed rapparree Gregory Costigan, and his two brothers, took refuge from the forces of Sir Charles Coote.

Gregory was betrayed to Coote by his fellow rapparree and kinsman Sean Geawr who led him into a trap at Gortnagloch (3km from here) where he was shot and beheaded on a sharp edged, upright flagstone, which projects about half a metre above ground and is still known as 'Gregory's Stone'.

His head was taken on the point of a spear to Coote's residence at Rushall. Coote's wife, who had been a friend of Gregory Costigan, was so shocked at the sight that she left Rushall Court and never returned to the residence.

__About 300m farther on, at a junction, keep left along the forest road which enters into the plantation. The road continues downhill to another junction,__ in the middle of which is the last remnant of a farm which was located here. This was an outhouse of the farm. The other buildings have disappeared under the forestry ploughs.

Keep to the right, and continue downhill, with the stream, through the beech trees, to the start.

COMMON SHREW *Often seen in the headlights of a car as it scurries to and fro in the roadway.*

FURTHER READING

'The Landscape of Slieve Bloom' by John Feehan.
Published by Blackwater Press
ISBN 0-905471-11-3

'Reading the Irish Landscape' by Frank Mitchell
Published by Country House
ISBN 0-946172-06-4

'Wild Flowers of Britain' by Roger Phillips
Published by Pan
ISBN 0-7063-5580-6

'Grasses, Ferns, Mosses and Lichens
of Great Britain and Ireland' by Roger Phillips
Published by Pan
ISBN 0-330-25959-8

'Animal Tracks and Traces' by Miroslav Bouchne
Published by Octopus
ISBN 0-7046-1486-1

'An Irish Beast Book' by James Fairley
Published by Blackstaff Press
ISBN 0-85640-314-8